ARISTOTLE

Corporate Terms Explained

Using Simple Analogies and Scenarios 5th-Grade Kids Can Easily Understand

MARBLE *Publishers*
ETERNAL PROSE

This book is dedicated to my two beautiful children,

Isabelle and Ris.

–Aristotle

Contents

1

Introduction For Parents and Educators

"Corporate Terms Explained: Using Simple Analogies and Scenarios 5th-Grade Kids Can Easily Understand" is here to demystify the often confusing world of business terms for young minds. In today's world, understanding how companies work is just as important as understanding money. This book is designed to make these complex ideas not only accessible but also enjoyable for your young readers.

Much like "Financial Terms Explained," this book uses relatable stories and analogies to bring corporate concepts to life. These scenarios are carefully crafted to engage both kids and adults, ensuring that everyone can grasp the simplicity behind these sometimes tricky terms.

You might wonder why a book about corporate terms belongs in a classroom or library. Well, just like with finances, having a solid understanding of how businesses operate is an essential skill. This book breaks down those barriers and makes these ideas clear and approachable.

As the author, I wish I had a resource like this when I was growing up. Traditional business literature is usually written for adults, which can be overwhelming for young readers. *"Corporate Terms Explained"* is different. It's meant to grab the attention of young minds and encourage them to explore its pages over and over again.

But this book offers more than just knowledge. It has the potential to inspire creativity and innovation. It might even spark ideas for new games or activities that incorporate these important business principles.

Whether you're reading this book with your child or they're exploring it on their own, you're in for a treat. Get ready for engaging stories that will not only entertain but also provide practical lessons. Together, let's embark on a journey towards understanding how businesses work, making sure the next generation is well-equipped to tackle the complexities of the corporate world.

Welcome to "*Corporate Terms Explained.*" Get ready for a fun and educational adventure!

2

Introduction For Students and Young Adults

Hey future business whiz!

First off, major kudos for snagging this awesome book. You're in for a real treat! Why? Because the person who handed this to you knows just how important it is to understand the ins and outs of the business world. And they believe this book will set you on the path to becoming a true business expert. How cool is that?

Imagine this: You're in high school or college, and your peers are struggling with all these tricky business terms. But not you! You mastered them back when you were just 10! How empowering would that be? You'd be the go-to person, the real guru, the one who makes complicated things seem like a breeze.

We call folks like you SMEs - Subject Matter Experts. And let me tell you, it's a pretty awesome title to have. It means you're the one who really knows your stuff. So get ready, because this book is your secret weapon to becoming a true business master.

You're about to embark on an exhilarating journey filled with puzzles, mini-businesses, and more. We're going to turn learning about business into a treasure hunt! Ever dreamed of running your own little enterprise, like a lemonade stand? Or making money grow like magic? Well, get set to do all that and more!

And here's the best part - you can share your newfound business smarts with your family and friends. They'll be super proud of you for being so savvy with your business knowledge.

So, are you geared up to dive into this business adventure? Grab this book, locate your favorite reading spot, and let's set off on a journey that'll transform you into a business superstar! Trust me, even the grown-ups will be blown away by what you learn from this book, so you'll have loads to chat about together. Let's get cracking!

3

A, B, C - Corporate Terms

360-Degree Feedback

Imagine you're playing a team sport like soccer. When the game is over, it's not just your coach who tells you how you played. Your teammates, the players on the other team, and even your parents watching from the sidelines all share their thoughts on how you did. This way, you get feedback from all angles - like a full circle - to help you become an even better player.

360-degree feedback in a company is similar. Instead of just your boss telling you how you're doing, it's everyone around you - your co-workers, teammates, and sometimes even the people you supervise - all giving their opinions. This helps you know what you're doing well and where you can improve, just like in soccer!

Accounts Payable (AP)

Think of accounts payable like a 'Thank You' card list. When you have a birthday party, your friends give you presents, right? After the party, you want to make sure you send them a 'Thank You' card. But first, you need to write down who gave you what. That list is a bit like accounts payable.

So, accounts payable is like keeping track of all the 'Thank You' cards you need to send out after a fun event, but instead of gifts, it's about keeping track of the things a company owes to different people or businesses. It's like a grown-up version of saying 'Thank You'!

Accounts Receivable (AR)

Accounts receivable is like having a piggy bank. You know how sometimes your grandparents or other relatives give you money as a gift? You put it in your piggy bank, and you know that someday you can use that money to buy something special you really want.

For companies, accounts receivable is a bit like their piggy bank. When they do work for someone, they send a bill, just like when you tell your parents about something you want to buy. The company waits for the money to come in, just like you wait for your piggy bank to fill up. Once the money is in, the company can use it to do more things and grow, just like you can use your piggy bank money to buy something special!

Action Item

Imagine you're a superhero getting ready for a big adventure. Each piece of your superhero gear, like your cape, mask, and boots, is like an "action item." They're all important parts of your outfit that you need to check off your list before you can go out and save the day. Just like in business, where there are different tasks to complete before you can achieve a big goal, being a superhero means taking care of your "action items" so you're prepared for any mission that comes your way!

Adjustable-Rate Mortgage (ARM)

Imagine you have a special kind of bicycle that can change how fast it goes. Let's say you're riding uphill, and it's really tough, so you make it go slow. But then, when you're on flat ground or going downhill, you make it go faster. An Adjustable-Rate Mortgage is a bit like that. It's a special kind of loan for a house where, instead of always paying the same amount every month, sometimes you might pay a little less, and sometimes a little more, depending on what's happening with interest rates. It's like changing the speed of your bike to match the road you're on!

Agile Methodology

Think of Agile Methodology like building a LEGO castle. Instead of trying to plan out the entire castle at once, you start by building smaller sections, like towers and walls. As you go, you can change and add things based on how you want your castle to look.

Agile in business is kind of like that. Instead of planning everything out right at the start, companies use Agile to work on smaller parts of a project and then make changes as they go along. It's like building a project brick by brick, so it turns out just the way you want it!

Agile Organization

Picture an Agile Organization like a team of skilled explorers in a magical forest. They don't follow just one path; instead, they have a map with lots of options. They can choose the best path based on what they discover along the way. If they find a bridge, they might use it. If they see a hidden cave, they might explore it.

In a company, being 'agile' is a bit like those explorers. They have a plan, but if they find a better way to do things, they're ready to change. It's like using a treasure map and being open to finding even more exciting treasures along the journey!

Alignment

Alright, imagine you and your friends want to build a super tall tower using your building blocks. For the tower to stand really tall and strong, all the blocks need to be perfectly lined up, just like "alignment" in the corporate world. It's like when everyone in a team or company works together in the same direction towards a common goal. Just as your tower needs every block to be in the right place, in business, everyone needs to be "aligned" to achieve success together!

Amortization

Imagine you have a giant chocolate bar, but you want to share it with your friends over several days. So, instead of eating it all at once, you decide to cut a small piece each day. This way, you get to enjoy it for a longer time.

Amortization in business is a bit like that. It's a way for companies to spread out the cost of something over time. Like your chocolate bar, they might have something big, like a machine or a building, and instead of paying for it all at once, they pay a little bit each month. This helps them manage their money smartly and enjoy the benefits of what they bought over a longer period.

Angel Investor

Think of an Angel Investor like a kind-hearted wizard in a fairy tale. When a young hero or heroine needs help on their quest, the wizard steps in with magical gifts or guidance. The wizard believes in the hero's potential and wants to see them succeed.

In the business world, an Angel Investor is a bit like that wizard. They're someone who believes in a small company or a new idea and gives them the support they need. Instead of magic, they use their money and advice to help the company grow and succeed, just like the wizard helps the hero on their journey!

Anti-Corruption

Imagine you and your friends are playing a game. In this game, everyone agrees to play by the rules and not cheat. If someone tries to break the rules and cheat, it wouldn't be fair, right?

Well, in the business world, there's a rule called "Anti-Corruption." It's like a big sign that says, "No Cheating Allowed!" Companies that follow this rule promise not to take shortcuts or do sneaky things to get ahead. They want to make sure everything is fair and honest, just like in our game. This way, everyone can trust them, and they can do business in a good and fair way!

Appraisal

Think of an appraisal like when you have a collection of your favorite trading cards, and you want to know how much they're worth. You ask an expert, like a collector or a card shop owner, to look at your cards and tell you their value. They carefully examine each card and consider things like rarity, condition, and demand. Once they're done, they give you a fair estimate of how much your collection is worth. So, in the corporate world, an appraisal is like getting an expert's opinion on how much something, like a house or a business, is worth. They carefully evaluate it and give you their best estimate of its value.

Appraised Value

Imagine you have a bunch of really cool action figures. Each one is different, and some might be super rare and special. Now, let's say you want to know how much they're all worth. So, you invite a superhero expert over, someone who knows all about action figures. They carefully look at each one, checking out how unique and well-kept they are. After inspecting everything, they tell you how much they think your entire action figure collection is worth.

In the grown-up world, an appraised value is like having a special expert determine how much something, like a house or a piece of art, is worth after carefully examining it and considering all its special qualities.

Assessed Value

Imagine you have a super-duper rare trading card, like one of those really cool ones you love to collect. Now, let's say you want to know how much it's worth. You call over a trading card expert, someone who knows all about these things. They carefully examine the card, looking at things like how rare it is and if it's in good condition. After checking everything out, they tell you how much they think your card is worth.

In the grown-up world, an assessed value is like having a special expert figure out how much something, like a house or a piece of property, is worth after carefully examining it and considering all its special qualities. They look at things like how big it is, where it's located, and what condition it's in.

Assessor

Let's pretend you have a super fun puzzle. But, there's a catch! This puzzle is a bit tricky and you need someone who's really good at puzzles to help you out. So, you invite over your friend who's like a puzzle expert. They're amazing at figuring out all the little details and finding where each piece fits. They're like a puzzle "assessor" because they're the go-to person for understanding how all the pieces fit together.

In the grown-up world, an assessor is like a super skilled expert who's really good at figuring out how much something is worth or understanding all the details about a particular situation, like the value of a house or a piece of land. They're the go-to people for getting a clear picture of things.

B Corporation (Benefit Corporation)

Imagine you have a superhero team, but instead of just fighting bad guys, they also really care about the environment and helping others. They make sure that while they're saving the day, they're also doing good things for the planet and the community. So, they're not just regular heroes, they're "Benefit Superheroes" or "B Heroes" for short!

In the grown-up world, a B Corporation, or Benefit Corporation, is a special kind of company that's like those superheroes. They don't just focus on making money, they also have a big mission to do good for the world, like helping the environment or supporting their local communities. They want to be heroes for the planet and for people!

Balance of Trade

Think of the Balance of Trade like a big trading card game. Imagine you and your friend are playing, and you both have different cards. Sometimes, you trade cards with each other. If you trade a rare card for a common one, you might not feel like it's a fair trade.

The Balance of Trade in a country is a bit like that. It's like keeping track of all the trades your country makes with other countries. If your country trades more valuable things for less valuable things, it's like trading a rare card for a common one. The Balance of Trade helps figure out if your country is making good trades or if it needs to adjust its strategy in the trading game!

Balance Sheet

Think of a Balance Sheet like a snapshot of a lemonade stand's belongings. On one side, you have all the lemons, sugar, cups, and money you've collected. On the other side, you have the lemonade you've made and the money you spent to get everything.

If you count everything up, both sides should be equal. That way, you know how much lemonade you can make and how much you have left over. In a company, a Balance Sheet is like a big lemonade stand report. It shows all the things they own and how much they owe, so they can make sure everything adds up just right!

Bandwidth

Imagine you have a big plate of cookies in front of you. Each cookie represents a different task or job you have to do. Now, if your plate is already full of cookies, you might not have enough "bandwidth" to take on another task. It's like saying you don't have enough room on your plate for another cookie. In the corporate world, "bandwidth" means how much time and capacity you have to take on new projects or tasks without feeling overwhelmed. Just like with cookies, you need to make sure you have enough space on your plate for everything you want to accomplish!

Bankruptcy Law Firms

Let's pretend you have a team of wizards who are really good at fixing things when they go wrong. But sometimes, things go really, really wrong in a magical land, and some wizards specialize in fixing those big, tricky problems. They're like the special team of wizards who help when things get super tough.

Well, in the adult world, there are special teams of lawyers who help when companies or people have really big financial problems. These lawyers are like the wizard team for money problems, and they work at places called "Bankruptcy Law Firms". They're experts at figuring out how to make things right when money things get really, really tough!

Benchmarking

Imagine you and your friends are having a race. Each of you wants to see who can run the fastest. To know how well you did, you might look at the fastest time any of you have ever run before. This previous best time becomes the "benchmark" for your race. In the corporate world, "benchmarking" is like comparing how well your company is doing compared to others. It's like seeing how fast you can run compared to your previous best time. It helps businesses see where they stand in the competition and find ways to improve!

Best Practice

Think of a best practice like a set of instructions for building an awesome treehouse. When you follow these instructions, you end up with a treehouse that's safe, sturdy, and loads of fun! In the corporate world, a "best practice" is like a set of instructions or methods that businesses follow to do things the most effective and successful way. It's like having a guidebook to help them build their own successful "treehouses" or projects!

Bill of Materials (BOM)

Think of a Bill of Materials like a recipe for building a cool LEGO spaceship. When you want to build it, you don't just start putting pieces together randomly. You follow a special list that tells you which pieces you need and how many of each.

In the business world, a Bill of Materials is like that LEGO recipe. It's a special list that tells the company all the parts they need to make something, like a car or a computer. This way, they can make sure they have everything they need before they start building, just like you do with your LEGO spaceship!

Bleeding Edge

Imagine you and your friends are playing a brand-new game. It's so new that you're the first ones to try it out. This game has the coolest, most exciting features that no other game has. You're on the "bleeding edge" of fun and adventure!

In the corporate world, being on the "bleeding edge" means using the very latest and most advanced technology or ideas. It's like having access to the newest, most amazing game that no one else has played yet. Companies that are on the "bleeding edge" are always looking for the most innovative and exciting ways to do things!

Blockchain Technology

Imagine you have a magic notebook that records every adventure you go on, and once you write something in it, you can't change it. You can share this notebook with your friends, and they can add their own adventures too. This notebook is so special that everyone trusts it, and no one can make up fake stories.

Blockchain technology is a bit like that magic notebook. It's a special way of keeping records that's super safe and everyone can trust. People use it for all sorts of things, like keeping track of money or sharing important information. Once something is written in the 'magic notebook,' it's there for everyone to see and no one can change it. It's like having a super secure diary for important grown-up stuff!

Blue Collared Worker

Let's imagine a big construction site with workers wearing their sturdy blue collared shirts. These workers are like the heroes of building things. They use tools like hammers, saws, and drills to put together houses, bridges, and all sorts of amazing structures.

Now, think of them as the action heroes of a team. They're the ones who turn plans and designs into real, tangible things. Just like in a superhero movie, they're the ones doing the heavy lifting and making sure everything is strong and safe.

So, when we talk about a "blue collared worker" in the grown-up world, we're talking about people who use their hands and tools to build and create things. They're the ones who help turn ideas into reality, just like our action heroes on the construction site!

Board of Directors

Let's picture a big ship sailing on the ocean. This ship is like a company, and it's headed towards success. But guess who's in charge of steering this ship and making sure it goes the right way? It's the "Board of Directors."

Now, think of the Board of Directors as a team of wise captains. Each captain has their own special knowledge and skills. One might know a lot about money, another might be really good at planning, and another might understand how to make the ship's crew work together smoothly.

These captains gather together regularly to talk about the best route for the ship. They make important decisions to make sure the ship (or company) keeps sailing in the right direction. They're like the guardians of the company, always looking out for what's best to help it succeed!

Boardroom

Alright, imagine the boardroom as the heart of a big treehouse. This treehouse is where all the important decisions are made for a special club. Inside the treehouse, there's a big table where the members of the club gather.

Now, think of the boardroom like the center of this treehouse. It's where everyone comes together to share their ideas and make important plans. The walls might have drawings and charts, just like the treehouse has cool decorations.

The boardroom is where grown-ups in a company gather to discuss important things about the business. It's like their clubhouse, but instead of planning treehouse adventures, they're planning how to make their company even better!

Brainstorm

Imagine you and your friends are planning the ultimate adventure. Each of you comes up with awesome ideas on where to go and what to do. You're all throwing out exciting suggestions, like going on a treasure hunt or having a super cool picnic in a secret forest. This big, creative sharing of ideas is just like a "brainstorm" in the corporate world.

In a company, when people have a "brainstorm," they gather together to share all kinds of exciting ideas for a project or a problem they're trying to solve. It's like having a big adventure planning session, but for work! Everyone pitches in their unique and awesome ideas, just like you and your friends planning that ultimate adventure!

Brand Equity

Think of brand equity like a favorite video game character. When you play a game with that character, you know they're really good at certain things, and you trust them to help you win. You might even want to buy toys or clothes with that character on them because you like them so much.

In the business world, brand equity is a bit like having a popular video game character. When people see a certain brand, they trust it to be good quality and they like it. They might even choose that brand over others because they trust it. It's like when you choose to play a game with your favorite character because you know they're awesome!

Brand Extension

Imagine you have a favorite superhero comic book. You love reading about their adventures and all the cool things they do. Now, imagine if that superhero decided to try something new, like starting their own line of action figures or making their own video game. It's still connected to the superhero, but it's a different way for fans to enjoy and interact with their favorite character.

Brand extension in business is a bit like that. It's when a company takes something they're really good at and tries something new that's related. For example, if a company is known for making tasty snacks, they might try making a new type of snack that's a little different. It's a way for them to offer something new and exciting to their customers, but still connected to what they're known for.

Brand Image

Think of a brand image like a superhero's costume. When you see a superhero in their special outfit, you know who they are and what they stand for. Spider-Man wears his red and blue suit, and you instantly know he's here to save the day.

In the business world, a brand image is a bit like a superhero's costume. It's what a company wears to show the world who they are. It includes their logo, colors, and the way they present themselves. Just like you trust a superhero when you see them in their costume, people trust a company when they see their brand image. It tells them what kind of company it is and what they can expect.

Branding

Think of branding like a superhero's symbol. When you see Batman's bat symbol in the sky, you know he's on his way to save Gotham City. It's a special sign that represents who he is and what he stands for.

In the business world, branding is a bit like a company's special symbol. It's not just a logo, it's everything that makes a company unique. It's the colors, the pictures, the way they talk, and the feeling you get when you think about them. Just like Batman's symbol tells you he's coming to save the day, a company's branding tells you what they're all about and why you should trust them.

Break-Even Point

Think of a Break-Even Point like a lemonade stand. Imagine you have a stand where you sell cups of lemonade. You had to buy lemons, sugar, cups, and a table to set up your stand. Each cup of lemonade you sell helps you earn some money back.

The Break-Even Point is like the moment when you've sold just enough cups of lemonade to cover all the things you bought to start the stand. It's the point where you haven't made a profit yet, but you also haven't lost any money. After the Break-Even Point, every cup of lemonade you sell is like pure profit because you've already covered your initial costs.

Broker

Imagine you have a friend who's really good at trading stickers. They know which stickers are super rare and which ones lots of people want. So, when you want to swap stickers with someone, you go to your friend because they can help you get the best deal.

Well, in the grown-up world, there are people called "Brokers" who are like super skilled sticker-traders, but with things like stocks, houses, or even art! They help match up buyers and sellers, making sure everyone gets a fair and square deal.

Brokerage

Imagine you have a big box of toys, and you want to trade some of them with your friends. But it's not easy to find the right friends who want exactly what you have and have what you want. That's where a "brokerage" comes in.

A brokerage is like a magical market where kids come together to trade their toys. There are experts called "brokers" who help match up kids who want to trade, making sure everyone gets something they're really excited about! So, it's like having a toy trading party with a special helper to make sure everyone leaves happy. In the grown-up world, brokerages help people trade things like stocks, houses, and other valuable stuff!

Burn Rate

Think of a Burn Rate like a race car's fuel gauge. When you start a race, the gauge shows a full tank of gas. As you zoom around the track, the needle slowly moves down because you're using up the fuel. The Burn Rate is how fast you're using up the gas.

In business, the Burn Rate is kind of like the fuel gauge for a company. It shows how quickly they're using up their money to run the business. If they're spending money really fast, it's like the needle on the gauge dropping quickly. If they're spending more slowly, it's like the needle moving down more slowly. It helps the company keep track of how long their 'race' can last before they need to refuel!

Business Ethics

Let's picture business ethics like the rules of a game, but not just any game - a super important game where everyone wants to play fair and have fun.

Imagine you and your friends are playing a game together. Now, if someone tries to cheat or do something sneaky, it wouldn't be much fun, would it? That's why you all agree on certain rules to make sure everyone has a fair chance to win.

Business ethics are like those rules, but for grown-ups who run companies. They're the guidelines that help them make sure everything is fair and honest in the world of business. Just like in our game, it's important for everyone to follow these rules so that the game - or in this case, the business - can run smoothly and everyone can be successful.

Business Model

Let's think of a business model like a recipe for making your favorite dessert. You know how you gather ingredients like flour, sugar, eggs, and chocolate chips? Each ingredient plays a specific role, right?

In a business model, it's kind of the same idea. Instead of ingredients, you have different parts that work together to make a business successful. There's the part that decides what the business will sell (like cupcakes or toys), how it will sell them (like in a store or online), and how it will make money.

Just like a good recipe, a well-thought-out business model helps the business grow and be successful. It's like having all the right steps to bake a delicious cake - when everything is in place, it turns out just right!

Business Process Improvement (BPI)

Think of Business Process Improvement like leveling up in a video game. When you start, you might not be very good at certain challenges. But as you practice and learn new strategies, you get better and better. Eventually, you can breeze through those challenges that used to be really hard!

In a company, Business Process Improvement is a bit like leveling up. They look at how they do things and figure out smarter and more efficient ways to get tasks done. It's like finding the best moves in a game so you can conquer any challenge that comes your way!

Business Process Optimization

Let's imagine you're playing a game with building blocks. You have a big pile of blocks, and you want to build the tallest tower possible. But here's the catch - you have to do it in a certain amount of time.

Now, you can start by stacking blocks one by one, but that takes a lot of time and might not get you the tallest tower. So, what do you do? You figure out a way to stack the blocks faster and more efficiently.

That's a bit like business process optimization. In a company, there are many tasks and steps to get things done, just like stacking blocks. Business process optimization is like finding the fastest and most efficient way to do those tasks, so the company can be really successful and efficient. It's like building the tallest tower of blocks, but in the business world!

Business Process Reengineering (BPR)

Imagine you have a big LEGO castle that you've built over time. But now, you want to make it even cooler and more efficient. So, instead of just adding more pieces, you take it apart and rebuild it from scratch. This way, you can make it stronger, faster, and even more awesome!

In a company, Business Process Reengineering is a bit like rebuilding a LEGO castle. Instead of just making small changes here and there, they completely rethink and rebuild how they do things. This helps them become much better at what they do, just like your LEGO castle becomes even more amazing after you reengineer it!

Buyer's Agent

Let's say you're going on a grand adventure to explore a mysterious forest, but you've never been there before. You're excited, but you're a bit nervous too because you want to make sure you find all the hidden treasures and avoid any tricky traps. That's where a "buyer's agent" comes in.

A buyer's agent is like having a trusty guide who knows the forest like the back of their hand. They're there to help you find the best paths, point out the cool stuff, and make sure you don't stumble into any sticky situations. They're on your team, making sure you have the most epic adventure possible! In the grown-up world, a buyer's agent helps people find and buy the perfect houses, making sure they get the best deal and avoid any hidden surprises.

Buy-In

Let's say you and your friends want to have a super fun day together. Each of you has a different idea of what to do. One friend suggests going to the amusement park, another wants to have a giant water balloon fight, and someone else wants to build an awesome fort.

Now, before you can decide what to do, everyone needs to agree on one idea. So, you all start talking and sharing why you think your idea is the best. After a while, you notice that everyone is starting to get excited about going to the amusement park. They're all saying things like, "Yeah, we'll get to ride the roller coasters!" and "I love cotton candy!"

That's when you realize everyone is on board with the amusement park idea. They've all given their agreement and are really looking forward to it. In the corporate world, when everyone agrees and supports a plan or an idea, we call it "buy-in." It's like when you and your friends all agree on going to the amusement park because it's the most exciting option for everyone!

C Corporation (C Corp)

Let's pretend that a "C Corporation" is like a big pizza party organizer. Imagine you and your friends decide to have a massive pizza party with lots of different pizzas, toppings, and fun activities.

Now, the person who's in charge of planning everything, like ordering the pizzas, setting up games, and making sure everyone has a great time, is like the "C Corporation." They take care of all the important details, just like the party organizer.

But here's the cool part: if anything goes wrong at the party, like if someone spills a drink or accidentally knocks over the game pieces, the party organizer (C Corporation) is responsible for fixing it. They handle all the cleanup and make sure the party keeps running smoothly.

So, think of a C Corporation as the ultimate party planner for big businesses, making sure everything is organized, fun, and that any messes get cleaned up!

Capital Expenditure (CapEx)

Think of a Capital Expenditure like building a treehouse. You need to gather all the wood, nails, and other materials to make it sturdy and safe. These things cost money, but once you have them, you can enjoy your treehouse for a long time.

In a company, a Capital Expenditure is like building something special that they'll use for a long time. It could be a new building, like an office, or big machines to help them make things faster. They spend money upfront, but it's an investment in making their business even better in the future, just like building a treehouse for years of fun!

Capital Gain

Imagine you have a collection of trading cards, and you decided to sell one of them because it's become really rare and valuable. You originally got that card for just a small amount of pocket money, but when you sell it, you get a lot more money in return. The extra money you make from selling the card, that's more than what you spent to get it, is a "capital gain."

So, a capital gain is like making extra money when you sell something that has become more valuable over time, just like your trading card!

Capital Structure

Let's imagine a big tower made of different kinds of building blocks. Each kind of block is like a different part of a company's money. Some blocks are like money the company borrowed, and others are like money the company got from selling its own pieces.

Now, just like in our tower, if we use too many of one kind of block and not enough of another, our tower might get wobbly and fall over. That's why companies need to think really carefully about how they use different kinds of money to build their "financial tower". This mix of different kinds of money is what we call the company's "capital structure". It's like figuring out the best combination of blocks to make the tallest, sturdiest tower.

Career Development Plan

Think of a Career Development Plan like a treasure map for your dream job. Imagine you want to become a space explorer. You don't just jump into a rocket and hope for the best. Instead, you create a special map with all the steps you need to take - like studying science, learning to fly a spaceship, and getting fit and strong.

In the grown-up world, a Career Development Plan is a bit like that treasure map. It's a special plan that helps you figure out the steps you need to take to reach your dream job. It might include things like going to school, learning new skills, and gaining experience in different places. It's like having a guide to help you become the amazing space explorer you want to be!

Cascade

Imagine you have a really big tower of building blocks. It's so tall that you can't reach the top! Now, you want to make sure all the blocks are stable and won't fall over.

So, you start at the very top and carefully push one block. That block gently nudges the next one, and then the next, like a line of dominoes. Soon, all the blocks are following each other, falling in a neat and controlled way, until they're all safely on the ground.

In the corporate world, a "cascade" is a bit like this. It means passing down information or instructions from the top leaders to the people below in a way that's organized and efficient, just like making sure all the blocks in your tower reach the ground without tumbling over!

Cash Burn

Think of Cash Burn like the allowance you get every week. Imagine you have a set amount of money to spend on things you want, like toys, games, or snacks. As the week goes on, you spend some of it, and you can see how much is left by counting your money.

In a business, Cash Burn is similar. It's like the money they have to spend on things they need to run the company, like paying employees, buying supplies, and other important stuff. They keep track of how much they spend, just like you keep track of your allowance. Knowing their Cash Burn helps companies make sure they have enough money to keep going and growing!

Cash Conversion Cycle

Think of a Cash Conversion Cycle like a relay race. You know how in a relay, runners pass a baton to each other? Each runner has to be quick and smooth to make sure they don't drop the baton or slow down the team.

In business, a Cash Conversion Cycle is a bit like a relay race, but with money. It's about how fast a company can take the money they spent on making and selling things, and turn it back into more money. Just like in a relay, being fast and efficient is super important!

Cash Flow

Let's pretend you have a lemonade stand. You buy lemons, sugar, and cups, and you sell your delicious lemonade to your neighbors. Each time you sell a cup of lemonade, you get some money. That's like the flow of cash coming into your lemonade stand.

But, remember, you also spent money to buy the lemons, sugar, and cups. So, when you subtract what you spent from what you earned, you'll know how much money you actually made. That's like figuring out how much lemonade money you have left after buying all your supplies.

So, cash flow is like keeping track of how much money you're making and spending in your lemonade business. It helps you know if you're making a profit or if you need to adjust your prices or expenses to do better next time!

Cash Flow Analysis

Think of Cash Flow Analysis like a superhero's energy meter. When a superhero uses their powers, their energy goes down. But when they rest and recharge, their energy goes back up.

In business, Cash Flow Analysis is a bit like that energy meter. It helps a company see how much money is coming in and going out. Just like a superhero needs to manage their energy to keep saving the day, a company needs to manage their cash flow to keep running smoothly and growing strong!

Cash Flow Statement

Think of a Cash Flow Statement like a diary of your money adventures. Every time you get some allowance, spend it on snacks or save it for a big toy, you write it down. At the end of the week, you can see where your money went and how much you have left.

In a company, a Cash Flow Statement is a bit like your money diary. It helps them keep track of all the money coming in from selling things and going out for expenses like supplies, paying workers, and other important stuff. It's like a special report that tells the company how they're doing with their money adventures!

Certified (vs. Licensed)

Let's pretend you're a super skilled wizard with two kinds of magical scrolls. The first kind is a "Certified" scroll. These are like scrolls that your wise teacher has checked and said, "Yes, this magic is really good and safe to use."

The second kind is a "Licensed" scroll. These are like scrolls that you give special permission to your trusted friends to use. You tell them, "Okay, you can use this magic, but remember, it's important to be careful!"

So, when something is "Certified," it means an expert has looked at it and said it's top-notch. When something is "Licensed," it means you're giving special permission for someone to use it. Both are ways of saying, "This is good stuff, but let's be careful with it!"

Chain of Command

Think of a Chain of Command like a team of superheroes. In a superhero team, there's usually a leader, like the one who gives orders and makes sure everyone works together. Then, there are other heroes with different powers, each with their own role.

In a company, the Chain of Command is a bit like a superhero team. There are leaders, like bosses or managers, who make sure everyone knows what to do and keeps things running smoothly. Then there are different teams and workers, each with their own important jobs. Just like in a superhero team, everyone has a role to play in making sure the company achieves its goals!

Change Management

Think of Change Management like rearranging your bedroom. Imagine you've had your furniture in the same spots for a long time. But now, you want to change things up to make it feel more comfortable and fun. You plan where each piece should go, and then you work together with your parents to make it happen.

In a company, Change Management is a bit like rearranging a big office. When a company wants to make things better or more efficient, they plan out the changes they want to make. Then, they work with all the employees to help them adjust to the new way of doing things. It's like a team effort to create a better and more comfortable 'room' for everyone to work in!

Churn Rate

Think of Churn Rate like a game of musical chairs. You know how, when the music stops, someone is left without a chair? That person is 'out' of the game. In a way, the Churn Rate is like keeping track of how many times the music stops and someone has to leave.

In a business, Churn Rate is a bit like that game. It's about how many customers 'leave the game' or stop using a company's product or service. Just like in musical chairs, a company wants to make sure as few people as possible are 'out' so they can keep playing and having fun!

Circle Back

Imagine you're playing a game with your friends, and you need to make a decision. But, not everyone can agree on what to do next. So, you all decide to take a break and go do other things for a bit. Later, when you've all had some time to think and have more information, you come back together in a circle to talk about it again. It's like giving everyone a chance to have their say and come back with fresh ideas. In the corporate world, when someone says they need to "circle back," it means they want to take some time to think and discuss things more before making a final decision, just like in your game with your friends!

Circle of Influence

Let's imagine you have a special group of friends. Some of them are really good at certain games, like soccer or chess, while others are amazing at drawing or telling jokes. Now, when it comes to playing a game, you'd want to pick the friend who's great at that game, right? That's because you know they'll be a big help in winning.

In a company, people have their own special skills, just like your friends. Sometimes, when they need help or advice, they'll turn to the people they know are really good at that particular thing. That group of helpful, skillful people is like their "circle of influence." It's the people they trust and rely on to make things go smoothly, just like you rely on your talented friends for different games and activities!

Civil Rights Law Firms

Think of civil rights law firms like superheroes who use their special powers to make sure everyone is treated fairly and equally. Just like superheroes fight against villains to protect the city, civil rights law firms fight against discrimination and unfair treatment to protect the rights of people in our society. They use the law as their superpower to make the world a better and more just place for everyone.

Close Corporation

A close corporation is like a small clubhouse where only a few friends are allowed in. Imagine you and a few of your closest buddies have a special club with its own secret rules and games. It's exclusive and not open to everyone. Similarly, a close corporation is a small group of people who run a business together, and it's not open to the general public. They work closely together, like your close-knit group in the clubhouse!

Close the Loop

Let's pretend you're doing a puzzle, and there's just one piece missing. You search all over, and finally, you find it! You place it in, and now the puzzle is complete. You've "closed the loop" on your puzzle adventure.

In a company, sometimes people need to finish up a project or make sure everything is done just right. When they take care of that final piece or step, it's like closing the loop on their project. Everything is in place, and they can say, "We did it!" just like you do with your finished puzzle.

Closed Corporation (Private Corporation)

A closed corporation is a bit like a secret club where only certain friends are allowed. Think of it as having a treehouse in your backyard. Imagine that this treehouse is where you and a few of your closest friends have your own special club. You have secret meetings, make decisions together, and have fun playing games up there.

Now, not just anyone can come into your treehouse club. Only the friends you've chosen are allowed in. It's private and exclusive, just for you and your select group.

In the business world, a closed corporation is similar. It's a special kind of company where only a small group of people, like a few friends in your treehouse club, own and run the business. It's not open to the public to buy shares like some other companies. So, it's like having your own secret business club with a select group of members.

Closing

Alright, let's imagine you're at the finish line of a big race. You've been running really fast, and now you're about to cross the finish line. You can see the tape stretched out in front of you. When you burst through that tape, you know you've completed the race successfully.

In the world of business, a "closing" is a bit like that finish line moment. It's the very end of a deal or a sale. Imagine you've been working on a project or trying to sell something, and then, when everything is agreed upon and all the details are sorted out, you have a final meeting. This meeting is like bursting through the finish line tape. It means the deal is done, and everyone can celebrate their success!

Closing Costs

Let's picture this: You're getting ready for a big adventure. You've packed your bags, got your ticket, and you're all set to go. But before you can board the plane, you need to get a special pass to enter the airport. This pass costs a little bit of money, but it's necessary to start your exciting journey.

In the world of buying a house, "closing costs" are a bit like that special pass. When you're about to become the owner of a new home, there are some extra costs you need to pay at the very end. These costs help make sure everything is in order, like paperwork and fees for different services. It's like that special pass you need before starting your amazing adventure in your new house!

Code of Ethics

Imagine you and your friends are in a club where you have a special set of rules. These rules make sure everyone is fair, kind, and treats each other with respect. For example, no pushing, no taking things without asking, and always helping if someone needs it.

A company also has its own set of special rules called a "Code of Ethics." These rules make sure everyone who works there is fair, honest, and treats each other and their customers with respect, just like your club rules. So, if someone follows the Code of Ethics, it means they're doing their best to be a good and fair member of the company team!

Collaborate

Imagine you and your friends decide to build an amazing treehouse together. Each friend brings something special: one has great ideas, another brings the tools, and someone else helps with the decorations. You all work together, sharing your skills and ideas, to create the coolest treehouse ever! That's what it means for people in a company to collaborate. They work together, bringing their different talents and ideas to achieve something awesome!

Compensation Package

Think of a Compensation Package like a special meal deal at your favorite restaurant. Usually, when you order a meal, you get the main dish. But with a meal deal, you also get extra things like a drink, dessert, and maybe even a toy. It's a whole package of goodies!

In a job, a Compensation Package is a bit like a meal deal. Instead of just getting a paycheck, employees get extra benefits like health insurance, paid time off, and maybe even a bonus. It's like getting a whole bunch of extra goodies along with your salary to make working for the company even better!

Competitive Advantage

Think of a Competitive Advantage like having a special power in a video game. You know how some characters can run faster or jump higher? That gives them an advantage over the other players, and it helps them win the game.

In business, a Competitive Advantage is a bit like having a special power. It's something a company does or has that makes it better or different from other companies. It could be making really cool toys, having super-friendly customer service, or making things faster and cheaper. This special power helps the company stand out and be the best in the game of business!

Competitive Analysis

Imagine you're in a big game of hide-and-seek with your friends. Before you start hiding, you take a moment to watch how your friends hide. Some might find really good spots, while others might not hide as well. This way, when it's your turn to seek, you know where to look first.

In business, a Competitive Analysis is a bit like that game of hide-and-seek. Companies want to know how their competitors are doing. They watch what products they're selling, how they're marketing them, and how much they're charging. This helps them make their own strategies smarter, so they have a better chance of 'winning' in the business world!

Compliance

Think of Compliance like playing a board game with rules. Just like in Monopoly or Scrabble, there are specific rules you have to follow. If you try to make up your own rules, it wouldn't be fair or fun for everyone playing.

In business, Compliance is a bit like following the rules of a board game. Companies have to follow certain rules and laws to make sure everything is fair and safe for everyone involved. It's like making sure everyone is on the same page and playing by the same rules in the game of business!

Condominium (Condo)

Imagine if you and your friends decided to build a treehouse together. You all chip in some money to buy the materials and work together to build it. Now, even though you each own a part of the treehouse, you also have to take care of it together. That means you all help with repairs, cleaning, and making sure it's a nice place to hang out.

A condominium, or "condo" for short, is a bit like that treehouse. It's a building where different people own their own living spaces, like apartments, but they also share common areas like hallways, the yard, or a swimming pool. So, it's like owning your own part of a big clubhouse with your friends and taking care of it together.

Conflict of Interest

Imagine you and your friends are playing a game where you're all trying to win a prize. Now, imagine one of your friends is also the referee of the game. They have a special job to make sure everyone is playing fair and following the rules.

But what if your friend, the referee, really wants you to win because they're your best buddy? They might feel a little torn between being your friend and doing their job as the referee. That's a bit like a "conflict of interest" in the grown-up world.

In a company, people have their own jobs and responsibilities, just like your friend being the referee. Sometimes, they might have another role or a special connection that could make it tricky for them to make a fair decision. That's when they have to be really careful to make sure they're doing what's best for the company and everyone involved. It's a bit like making sure the game is fair, even when your friend really wants you to win!

Contingency

Let's say you and your friends plan a big picnic at the park. You check the weather forecast, and it says there might be rain. To be safe, you come up with a backup plan just in case. This backup plan could be going to an indoor play area or having a movie day at someone's house.

In the world of business, a "contingency" is like having a backup plan. It's something a company prepares in case something unexpected happens, so they're ready to handle it without too much trouble. Just like your backup plan for the picnic, it's a smart way to be prepared!

Continuous Improvement

Think of Continuous Improvement like practicing your favorite video game. When you first start, you might not be very good at it, but the more you play, the better you get. You learn new tricks, discover hidden paths, and figure out how to beat tough levels.

In business, Continuous Improvement is a bit like leveling up in a video game. Companies work to get better at what they do. They find smarter ways to work, learn from their mistakes, and come up with new and exciting ideas. It's like always striving to be the best player in the game of business!

Contract

Let's play a game! Imagine you have a super cool trading card. You really want a rare one that your friend has. So, you both decide to make a deal. You say, "I'll trade you my cool card for your rare one!"

Now, you both shake hands to seal the deal. That's like a "contract" for grown-ups. It's a special promise written down on paper, saying, "We agreed to do this!" Just like your trading card deal, a contract is a way for people to make sure everyone keeps their promises in important situations. Cool, right?

Cooperative (Co-op)

Imagine you and your friends really love playing soccer. Instead of joining an official soccer team with coaches, you decide to form your own little team. Each person has a special job, like someone brings snacks, another keeps

41

track of scores, and someone else makes sure everyone is playing fair. You all work together and make decisions as a team.

In a "cooperative" or "co-op" in the business world, it's like a special team of people who work together to make decisions and run a business. Each person has a role, and they all share in the responsibilities and rewards. It's like your soccer team, but for grown-ups in business!

Copyright

Imagine you draw a really cool picture of a dragon. It's so awesome that everyone wants a copy of it. But you want to make sure that only you get credit for your amazing artwork. So, you write your name on the bottom of the picture, kind of like signing it.

In the world of business, copyright is a bit like signing your artwork. It's a special way to say, 'Hey, I made this, and it's mine.' It helps creators, like artists, writers, and musicians, keep their work safe and make sure they get credit for it. So, just like you wouldn't want someone else to say they drew your dragon, creators use copyright to protect their amazing creations!

Core Competency

Think about a superhero team. Each hero has their own special power. One can fly, another is super strong, and someone else is really smart. When they work together, they're an unbeatable team because they each bring something unique to the table. In a company, the things it's really, really good at are its core competencies. It's like the special powers that make it stand out from other companies. They're the things the company does better than anyone else!

Core Values

Think of Core Values like the rules you and your friends have in your secret clubhouse. These rules make sure everyone is treated with kindness and respect, and they help make your clubhouse a fun and safe place to hang out.

In a company, Core Values are a bit like the rules of your secret clubhouse. They're the important beliefs that everyone in the company agrees to follow. These values guide how the company treats its employees, customers, and everyone else they interact with. They help create a positive and friendly environment, just like in your awesome clubhouse!

Corporate Culture

Let's pretend you have a big box of crayons, and you and your friends love to draw and create together. Now, imagine if you all had a special way of doing things, like always starting with a blue crayon or adding lots of sparkles.

That special way you all work and play together, that's a bit like what we call "corporate culture" in a company. It's like having a set of rules or traditions that make the company unique. Some companies might really like teamwork and always working together, while others might encourage lots of creativity and trying new things.

So, just like you and your friends have your own way of creating art, companies have their own way of doing things, and that's their "corporate culture." It's what makes each company special and different from others.

Corporate Governance

Let's imagine your school has a special team of students who help make sure everything runs smoothly. They might check that everyone's following the rules, organize fun events, and make sure everyone feels included and heard. These students are like the leaders who help guide and manage the school.

In a big company, there's something similar called "corporate governance." It's like having a team of really responsible adults who make sure everything in the company is fair and follows the rules. They help decide important things, like how the company should be run, and they make sure everyone, from the bosses to the regular employees, are treated fairly.

So, just like your school has its special team to make sure everything is fair and fun, companies have their own group of responsible adults to make sure everything is fair and follows the rules, and that's called "corporate governance." It's like having a team of grown-ups who help steer the company in the right direction.

Corporate Law Firms

Let's imagine you and your friends are building a really cool treehouse. But to make sure everything is safe and built the right way, you decide to ask your friend's older brother who knows a lot about building things. He's like the expert advisor on your treehouse project.

In the grown-up world, when people have big projects or need legal advice for their businesses, they might go to a "corporate law firm." It's like having a team of expert advisors who help make sure everything is done correctly and legally for their business projects, just like your friend's older brother helps make sure your treehouse is safe and sturdy.

Corporate Restructuring

Let's imagine you have a big box of building blocks. You've made a really cool tower, but then you get an idea. Instead of one tall tower, you want to make two smaller ones. So, you take apart some blocks and start building again.

Corporate restructuring is a bit like that. Imagine a big company is like a tower made of lots of different parts, like departments and teams. Sometimes, the people in charge might think it's a good idea to change how these parts are organized. They might decide to make new teams, combine some, or even move them around. It's like taking apart the tower and building something new and different.

So, corporate restructuring is when the big company decides to change how its different parts are organized, just like when you change how your building blocks are stacked to make something new and exciting!

Corporate Social Responsibility (CSR)

Imagine you and your friends have a treehouse. You all love playing in it, but you notice that some of the nearby trees are starting to look sick. So, you and your friends decide to take care of those trees. You water them, give them extra love, and make sure they're healthy again.

In the grown-up world, Corporate Social Responsibility is a bit like taking care of those trees. It's when a company looks around and sees how they can help their community and the environment. They might donate to charities, help clean up parks, or find other ways to make the world a better place. It's like the company's way of giving extra love and care to the world around them!

Corporation

Let's pretend you and your friends decide to start a super awesome club. This club is going to have rules, a clubhouse, and maybe even its own special handshake! But here's the thing, you want to make sure everyone in the club can share the responsibilities and the fun equally. So, you decide to make it a "corporation."

A corporation is like a big club where people work together to do special things. Each person in the corporation gets a say, and they all share the work and the good times. Just like in your club, everyone has a part to play!

Cost of Capital

Think of Cost of Capital like building a really cool treehouse. To make it awesome, you need the best materials like strong wood, sturdy nails, and maybe even a cool rope ladder. But these things cost money, so you need to figure out the best way to get them without spending too much.

In a company, Cost of Capital is a bit like figuring out how to get the best materials for your treehouse. It's about finding the right mix of money from different sources, like using your allowance, savings, or maybe even asking your friends to chip in. This way, you can build the coolest treehouse without spending too much!

Cost of Goods Sold (COGS)

Think of Cost of Goods Sold (COGS) like the ingredients you need to make a delicious batch of cookies. You need flour, sugar, chocolate chips, and butter. These are the things you spend money on to create your yummy treats.

In a business, Cost of Goods Sold is a bit like the ingredients for your cookies. It's the money a company spends on all the things they need to make and sell their products. So, if a company makes toys, the COGS would include the materials, like plastic and paint, that they use to make the toys. Just like you need the best ingredients for your cookies, a company needs good quality materials to make their products!

Cost-Benefit Analysis (CBA)

Imagine you have a tough decision to make: whether to spend your allowance on a cool new video game or save it for a big theme park trip with your friends. To figure out what's the best choice, you make a list of all the fun you'd have with the game and all the fun you'd have at the theme park. Then, you compare which one gives you the most fun for your allowance money.

In business, Cost-Benefit Analysis (CBA) is a bit like making that list. When a company has to make a big decision, they look at all the costs and all the benefits of each choice. It helps them figure out which option will bring them the most 'fun' or value for their investment. It's like being a smart spender, but for a whole company!

Criminal Defense Law Firms

Imagine you and your friends are playing a game, like a big game of tag. Now, in this game, there's a special person called the "defender." Their job is to help anyone who gets tagged unfairly. They're like the referee in a sports game, making sure everything is fair.

Criminal defense law firms are kind of like those special defenders in the game. They help people who are in trouble, making sure everything is fair and everyone gets a fair chance, just like in your game of tag. They're like the superheroes of the legal world!

Crisis Management

Imagine you're the captain of a ship on a big adventure. Suddenly, a storm comes out of nowhere! The wind is howling, and the waves are crashing. You have to steer the ship carefully, tell your crew what to do, and make sure everyone stays safe until the storm passes.

In business, Crisis Management is a bit like being the captain during a storm. Sometimes, unexpected problems or challenges come up, and a company needs to respond quickly and wisely. They have to make sure everyone is safe, figure out what to do, and guide the company through the tough times. It's like being a brave and smart captain during a storm in the business world!

Cross-Functional Team

Think of a Cross-Functional Team like a team of superheroes. Each superhero has their own special power, right? One can fly, another is super strong, and another can turn invisible. When they work together, they can solve all sorts of big problems!

In a company, a Cross-Functional Team is like a team of superheroes. Each member has their own special skills and knowledge, but they're from different parts of the company. When they come together to work on a project, they can use their unique abilities to solve really tough challenges. It's like a team of super-powered problem solvers!

Crowdfunding

Imagine you and your friends want to build the coolest treehouse ever, but you need some help getting all the awesome materials. So, you decide to ask everyone in the neighborhood if they'd like to chip in a little money. In return, they'll get a special pass to visit and play in your treehouse once it's built.

In business, crowdfunding is a bit like asking your neighbors for help with your treehouse. Companies might have a really cool idea, like a new kind of toy or game. They ask lots of people to contribute a little bit of money to help make it happen. In return, those supporters might get the first chance to play with the new toy or game when it's finished. It's like a big team effort to make something awesome!

Cryptocurrency

Imagine if you had a special kind of treasure that you could use to buy really cool stuff, but it wasn't made of gold or silver. Instead, it was made of virtual magic! This magic treasure is called cryptocurrency. It's like having your very own bag of wizard coins that you can use to trade for awesome things in a magical world of the internet.

In the grown-up world, cryptocurrency is a bit like having a magical currency for buying things online. It's not like the dollars and cents you use every day. Instead, it's a special kind of digital money that some people like to use for buying and trading. It's like being a wizard with your very own special coins!

Customer Acquisition Cost (CAC)

Think of Customer Acquisition Cost (CAC) like inviting friends to your awesome birthday party. You need to buy decorations, snacks, and maybe even plan some games. All of this costs money, but it's worth it because you'll have a fantastic time with your friends.

In business, Customer Acquisition Cost is a bit like planning your birthday party. Companies spend money on advertising, marketing, and sometimes even special offers to get new customers. It's an investment because once those customers come, they'll hopefully buy products or use services, making the company's party even more fun!

Customer Lifetime Value (CLV)

Imagine you have a favorite book series that you love reading. Each book in the series brings you hours of enjoyment and excitement. You know that you'll keep reading these books for a long time because you love them so much.

In business, Customer Lifetime Value (CLV) is a bit like how much joy you get from your favorite book series. Companies want to know how much value they get from a customer over a long time. If a customer keeps coming back and buying products or using services, they bring a lot of value to the company, just like your favorite books keep bringing you joy every time you read them!

Customer Relationship Management (CRM)

Think of Customer Relationship Management (CRM) like having a super organized clubhouse with a list of all your friends and their favorite games, snacks, and activities. This way, when your friends come over, you know exactly what they like and can make sure everyone has a great time.

In business, CRM is a bit like having a super organized system to keep track of all the customers and what they like. Companies use it to remember what products or services each customer prefers, how often they like to shop, and if they have any special requests. It helps make sure every customer has a fantastic experience, just like in your super organized clubhouse!

Customer Retention Rate

Imagine you have a treehouse club with your closest friends. Every week, you plan fun activities, like treasure hunts, games, and storytelling. You notice that the more fun and exciting activities you have, the more your friends want to come back to the treehouse.

In business, Customer Retention Rate is a bit like your treehouse club. It's about how many customers keep coming back to a company because they enjoy what the company offers. Just like in your club, when a company provides great products or services, customers want to keep coming back for more fun and excitement!

4

D, E, F - Corporate Terms

Days Payables Outstanding (DPO)

Think of Days Payables Outstanding (DPO) like a friendly neighborhood lemonade stand. When you buy a cup of lemonade, you promise to pay for it later. The lemonade stand owner keeps track of how many cups were sold but not yet paid for. They might even give you a special card that says how many cups you owe.

In business, DPO is a bit like the lemonade stand keeping track of how many cups of lemonade were sold but not yet paid for. It helps companies understand how much money they owe to their suppliers for things like ingredients or materials. Just like the lemonade stand owner, companies keep track of what's been sold and not yet paid for!

Days Sales Outstanding (DSO)

Imagine you have a lemonade stand, and you keep a special chart to note down who buys lemonade and when they promise to pay you. Some customers say they'll pay you tomorrow, while others might promise to pay in a few days. Your chart helps you keep track of when you can expect to receive the money.

In business, Days Sales Outstanding (DSO) is a bit like your special chart for the lemonade stand. It helps companies keep track of when their customers promise to pay for the products or services they've bought. This way, they know when to expect the money to come in, just like you do with your lemonade stand!

Debt Service Coverage Ratio (DSCR)

Think of Debt Service Coverage Ratio (DSCR) like a game of seesaw at the park. On one side, you have the money the company makes, and on the other side, you have the money they owe in loans. The seesaw needs to stay balanced, just like in the game. If one side has too much weight, it won't work properly.

In business, DSCR is a bit like the seesaw game. It helps companies see if they have enough money coming in to cover the money they owe in loans. If they have more money coming in, it helps keep things balanced. But if they owe too much and don't have enough coming in, it's like having too much weight on one side of the seesaw. It could cause problems!

Debt-to-Equity Ratio (D/E)

Think of a Debt-to-Equity Ratio (D/E) like building a sandcastle at the beach. When you build a sandcastle, you use two things: your own bucket of sand (that's your equity) and maybe some extra sand you borrow from your friend's bucket (that's the debt).

In business, the D/E ratio is a bit like making a sandcastle. It shows how much of the sandcastle is made from your own bucket of sand (equity) and how much is made from your friend's bucket (debt). Just like with your sandcastle, you want to make sure you have the right balance of sand (money) to build something strong and sturdy!

Decentralized Finance (DeFi)

Imagine you and your friends are playing a game of make-believe in a big park. Instead of having one person in charge and telling everyone what to do, you all work together and decide on the rules and roles. It's like a big team effort where everyone has a say.

In the world of money, Decentralized Finance (DeFi) is a bit like that make-believe game. Instead of one big bank or person being in charge of all the rules, lots of people work together using special computer programs. They decide on the rules for how money is used and shared. It's like a big team of people making financial decisions together!

Deed

Let's pretend you're the owner of a magical treehouse in the woods. Now, to prove that it's really yours, you have a special map. This map has your name on it, and it says that you're the true owner of the treehouse.

In the world of grown-ups and houses, that special map is like a "deed." It's a piece of paper that says, "This house belongs to you!" So, when someone has a deed, it means they're the real owner of a house or a piece of land, just like you with your magical treehouse!

Deep Dive

Imagine you have a big, mysterious treasure chest. It's locked tight, and you're really curious about what's inside. To find out, you'll need to do a "deep dive." This means you'll carefully examine every part of the chest, turning it over, looking at all the details, and maybe even using special tools to understand it fully.

In a company, doing a "deep dive" means looking very closely at something, like a project or a problem, to understand it as well as possible. It's like being a detective, studying every clue to solve a mystery!

Delegation

Think of delegation like being the captain of a spaceship. You have a team of astronauts, and each one has a special job. One astronaut is in charge of navigation, another takes care of communication, and so on. You trust your team to do their jobs well, so you can focus on being the best captain you can be.

In business, delegation is a bit like being the captain of a spaceship. The leader (like the captain) gives different tasks to team members who are best suited for them. This way, everyone can focus on what they're really good at, and the whole mission (or project) can be a success. It's like a well-organized space crew working together!

Deliverable

Let's imagine you're a detective, and you've been given a special mission to solve a mystery. Your "deliverable" in this case would be the final report you give to the chief of police. It's like the big envelope you hand over, filled with all the important clues, facts, and conclusions about the case. Just like you'd want that report to be clear and complete, in the corporate world, a "deliverable" is something you promise to give, like a report or a project, and it needs to be well-prepared and on time.

Depreciation

Think of depreciation like a magical spell that makes your toys a bit less shiny over time. When you get a new toy, it's super bright and exciting. But as you play with it and have lots of adventures, it starts to look a little worn out.

In business, depreciation is a bit like that magical spell. When a company buys things like machines or computers, they're super valuable and helpful. But as they're used over time, they become a bit less valuable because they get older or maybe a newer, better version comes out. It's like the natural wear and tear that happens with your toys, but with grown-up stuff!

Dilution

Let's imagine you have a big jar of delicious lemonade. It's just the right sweetness and tastes amazing. Now, if you decide to add some water to it, the lemonade won't be as strong and might taste a bit different.

Dilution in business is a bit like that lemonade. Imagine a company has a certain number of shares, and each share represents a piece of ownership. If the company decides to create more shares and sell them, it's like adding water to the lemonade. Each share becomes a bit less valuable because there are more of them.

So, dilution in business happens when a company creates more shares, which can affect how much each share is worth. It's like making the lemonade a bit lighter by adding more water.

Disruptive

Imagine you're playing a game of soccer with your friends. Everything's going smoothly, but suddenly someone introduces a new rule that allows players to use their hands. This totally changes how the game works, right? It's a bit surprising and shakes things up - that's what we mean by "disruptive" in the corporate world. It's like when a new idea or technology comes along that changes the way people usually do things. Just like the hand rule in soccer, it can be a big game-changer!

Disruptor

Imagine you're all playing a game of tag, but suddenly one of your friends brings out a secret weapon – a super speedy scooter! Now, the game is totally different because your friend can zoom around and tag everyone super fast. The scooter is the "disruptor" in the game because it changes how the game is played. In the corporate world, a disruptor is like a new idea, technology, or way of doing things that shakes up the usual way of doing business, just like that super speedy scooter changed your game of tag!

Diversification

Picture a basket of different fruits – apples, bananas, oranges, and grapes. Each fruit has its own special taste and texture, right? Now, imagine if you really, really liked apples, but that's all you had in your basket. If for some reason apples weren't available, you might be left without a snack you enjoy.

Diversification in business is a bit like having a basket with lots of different fruits. If one fruit isn't available or isn't doing so well, you still have others to enjoy. Similarly, in a business, if they're involved in different areas or industries, they're not relying too much on just one thing. This way, if one part of the business isn't doing so well, they have other parts that can still help them out.

So, diversification is like having a basket with a bunch of different fruits to make sure you always have something tasty to enjoy!

Diversity and Inclusion

Think of a garden with many different types of flowers and plants. Each one is unique and special in its own way. Some bloom in bright colors, others are tall, and some have beautiful fragrances. Together, they make the garden incredibly beautiful and interesting.

In a company, diversity and inclusion are a bit like having a garden with many different plants. It means having a team of people who come from all different backgrounds, have different talents, and bring their own special strengths. When everyone works together, it makes the company stronger and more creative, just like the beautiful garden with its unique flowers.

Dividend

Think of a dividend like the slices of a pizza. When you and your friends share a pizza, it's divided into equal parts so everyone gets a fair share. Some might like pepperoni, while others prefer cheese or veggies.

In business, a dividend is a bit like sharing a pizza. When a company makes a profit, they may decide to give a portion of it to the people who own a part of the company (called shareholders). Just like with the pizza, it's a way to make sure everyone gets a fair share of the good stuff!

Dividend Yield

Imagine you have a special plant in your garden that grows juicy, delicious fruits. Every year, this plant gives you a basket full of these yummy fruits. The amount of fruit you get compared to the size of the plant is called the 'fruit-to-plant size ratio'.

In business, dividend yield is a bit like that fruit-to-plant size ratio. It tells you how much 'fruit' (dividends) you get from your 'plant' (investment). If you have a big basket of dividends compared to the size of your investment, it's like having a really fruitful plant in your garden!

Down Payment

Let's imagine you're at a carnival, and there's this amazing roller coaster you really want to ride. The ticket to get on costs a bit more than you have in your pocket. So, you decide to make a deal with the carnival owner.

You say, "I'll give you some of my allowance now, and the rest when I get off the ride." It's like making a "down payment." You're putting some money down now to show you're serious, and you'll pay the rest later. Just like when you want to save your spot on a roller coaster, people make down payments when they want to save their spot on something special, like a house!

Drill Down

Let's say you have a big box of crayons, all mixed up in a pile. If you want to find a specific color, like your favorite shade of blue, you'll start by looking at the whole pile. But then, you decide to "drill down" and focus only on the blue crayons. Now, it's much easier to find exactly what you're looking for! In the corporate world, when people talk about "drilling down," they mean looking really closely at specific details or parts of a big project or idea, just like you did with the crayons to find your favorite blue!

Due Diligence

Imagine you're on a treasure hunt with your friends. Before you start digging for treasure, you need to look at maps, study clues, and make sure you're in the right spot. This careful planning and checking is like doing due diligence.

In business, due diligence is a bit like being a treasure hunter. Before a company makes a big decision, like buying another company or investing in a project, they do a lot of careful research and checking to make sure it's the right choice. It's like studying the maps and clues before you start digging for treasure!

Earnings Before Interest and Taxes (EBIT)

Think of Earnings Before Interest and Taxes (EBIT) like the money you make from your lemonade stand before you take out any costs. So, if you sell cups of lemonade for 50 cents each, and you've sold 20 cups, you've earned 10 dollars. That's your EBIT!

In business, EBIT is a bit like the money you make from selling your lemonade before you take out any costs like buying lemons or cups. It helps companies see how much they're making from their main business, before they consider other expenses. It's like counting your earnings from the lemonade stand before you think about how much it cost to make the lemonade.

Earnings Before Interest, Taxes, Depreciation, and Amortization (EBITDA)

Imagine you have a lemonade stand, but this time, you want to figure out how much money you're making after you've taken out all the costs. So, you count the money you earned, but you also subtract the money you spent on lemons, cups, and other supplies. The money left is what you get to keep for yourself. That's a bit like Earnings Before Interest, Taxes, Depreciation, and Amortization (EBITDA) in business.

In a company, EBITDA is a bit like figuring out how much money they're making from their main business, after they've taken out all the costs like supplies, equipment, and other important things. It helps them see how well they're doing without worrying about certain expenses. It's like counting how much money you get to keep from your lemonade stand after you've paid for all the things you needed to run it!

Earnings Per Share (EPS)

Think of Earnings Per Share (EPS) like a pizza that you and your friends share. You have a big pizza, and you want to make sure everyone gets a fair share. So, you cut it into equal slices, and each friend gets one. The more slices you have to share, the more each person gets.

In business, EPS is a bit like that pizza. The 'earnings' are the whole pizza, and the 'per share' part is how many slices (or shares) you divide it into. If a company makes a lot of money, and they have a lot of shares, then each share gets a bigger slice of the earnings pizza. It's a way of making sure everyone who owns a part of the company gets a fair share of the profits!

Easement

Let's imagine you have a big, beautiful treehouse in your backyard, but the only way to get to it is by walking through your neighbor's yard. Now, you don't want to keep asking your neighbor every time you want to visit your treehouse, right?

So, you talk to your neighbor and come up with an agreement. They give you a special path, like a little trail, that only you can use. This special path is like an "easement." It means you have permission to use that path to get to your treehouse without bothering your neighbor all the time. It's like having your very own secret trail!

Economic Value Added (EVA)

Imagine you have a lemonade stand and you've worked really hard to make it the best in town. You've spent money on lemons, cups, and your special secret recipe. After a day of selling lemonade, you count up all the money you made. But instead of just looking at the total, you also think about all the money you spent on supplies and how much time you put in.

In business, Economic Value Added (EVA) is a bit like that. It's about not only looking at how much money a company makes, but also thinking about all the costs and effort that went into making that money. It helps companies see if they're not just making money, but if they're making it in a smart and efficient way. It's like thinking about all the work you put into your lemonade stand to see if it was really worth it!

Ecosystem

Imagine you have a big, magical forest. In this forest, there are all sorts of plants and animals, like trees, flowers, birds, and butterflies. They all depend on each other to live happily. The trees provide homes for the birds, and the birds help spread seeds for new plants. It's like a big, natural team where everyone has a special job to do!

Now, think of a corporate ecosystem like a big, bustling city. There are different companies, just like there are different plants and animals in the forest. Some companies make things, like toys or clothes, while others help with services, like delivering packages or fixing computers. They all work together, each doing their own special thing, to make the city (or the corporate world) run smoothly!

Education Law Firms

Let's pretend you and your friends are part of a big club where you all learn new and exciting things together. Now, clubs need rules, right? That way, everyone knows how to play fair and have a good time.

But sometimes, there might be questions or disagreements about the rules. That's when you'd want a special group of people who really know the rules well. They're like the referees or captains of your club. They're the "Education Law Firms." They help make sure everyone is treated fairly and gets to learn and have fun together in the best way possible!

Elephant in the Room

Alright, imagine you and your friends are playing a game, and there's a big, colorful elephant sitting right in the middle of the play area. Everyone can see it, but for some reason, nobody talks about it! It's like the elephant is so big and obvious, but everyone pretends it's not there.

In the grown-up world, sometimes there are important things that everyone knows about, but they don't talk about them. It's like there's an "elephant in the room." It's a big topic that needs to be addressed, but for some reason, people avoid talking about it. It's kind of like when you have a big homework assignment and you keep putting it off, even though you know you need to do it!

Employee Benefits

Think of employee benefits like toppings on a pizza. When you order a pizza, you can choose to add extra cheese, pepperoni, veggies, and more. These toppings make the pizza even better and more enjoyable.

In a job, employee benefits are a bit like the extra toppings. They're the special things the company offers to make working there even better. This can include things like extra vacation days, health insurance, and sometimes even things like gym memberships. Just like with a pizza, these benefits make the job more enjoyable and rewarding for the employees!

Employee Engagement

Imagine you and your friends are putting on a play. Everyone has an important role to play, like acting, doing the costumes, and even designing the set. Now, imagine everyone is really excited about the play and gives their best effort to make it amazing. That's like employee engagement in a company.

In business, employee engagement is a bit like everyone being super excited and committed to doing their best at their jobs. Just like in the play, when everyone is giving their all, the whole production (or company) turns out better. It's when everyone is really involved and putting in their best effort to make the company successful!

Employee Onboarding

Think of employee onboarding like starting a new adventure in a video game. When you begin a new level, the game gives you all the tools, instructions, and a map to help you succeed. It helps you get familiar with the game world and sets you up for success.

In a company, employee onboarding is a bit like that. When someone joins a new company, they're starting a new 'level' in their career. The company gives them all the tools, information, and introductions they need to succeed in their new role. It's like the game's way of making sure you're set up for success in your new job adventure!

Employee Stock Ownership Plan (ESOP)

Imagine you and your friends decide to start a club together. To be a member, everyone chips in a little bit of money. With that money, you buy a special box of toys that all of you share and play with. Now, because everyone owns a part of the box, you all get to decide together which toys to play with and take turns having them.

In a company, an Employee Stock Ownership Plan (ESOP) is a bit like that club and special toy box. Instead of toys, it's like owning a little piece of the company. All the employees together own a part, and they get to make important decisions about the company. It's a way of saying, 'We're all in this together!'

Employee Turnover Rate

Think of the employee turnover rate like a game of musical chairs. Imagine you're at a party, and when the music stops, some of the players switch chairs. If this happens a lot, it means there's a high turnover rate. But if everyone stays in their chairs for a long time, the turnover rate is low.

In a company, the turnover rate is a bit like that game. It shows how many people leave their jobs and are replaced by new employees. If lots of people are switching 'chairs' (or jobs) frequently, the turnover rate is high. If people tend to stay in their 'chairs' for a long time, the turnover rate is low. It helps companies understand how stable their team is.

Employment Law Firms

Imagine you and your friends are playing a big game together. Everyone is excited and having fun, but sometimes, there might be disagreements about the rules or how to play fair. That's when you'd want a special group of people who know all the rules really well. They're like the referees or captains of your game. They're the "Employment Law Firms." They help make sure everyone at work is treated fairly and that the game (or the job!) is enjoyable for everyone involved!

Empowerment

Imagine you're the captain of a spaceship, and you have a crew of really smart and capable astronauts. You trust them to do their jobs and make decisions when you're not around. That's like empowerment in a company.

In business, empowerment means giving employees the trust, tools, and freedom to make decisions and take charge of their work. It's like saying, 'You're a capable astronaut, and I trust you to handle your responsibilities.' It helps make the team stronger and more successful!

Engagement

Imagine you're playing a really fun game with your friends. Everyone is excited and involved, talking, laughing, and having a great time. That feeling of everyone being so into the game and enjoying themselves is like "engagement" in the grown-up world.

In a company or a business, when people are engaged, it means they're really involved in their work. They're interested, enthusiastic, and they're doing their best to help the company succeed. It's like when you're so into a game that you give it your all and really try to win!

Entertainment Law Firms

Let's imagine you're all part of a big group putting on a play. There are actors, directors, and even people who handle the costumes and lights. But sometimes, there might be questions about who gets credit for what, or how the money from the tickets is shared. That's when you'd need some special helpers called "Entertainment Law Firms." They're like the backstage crew of your play, making sure everyone's treated fairly and that the show goes on smoothly!

Environmental Law Firms

Imagine you have a big garden with lots of different plants and flowers. Sometimes, you need to make sure that the soil is just right, and that the air and water are clean so everything can grow healthy and strong. That's where "Environmental Law Firms" come in. They're like the gardeners and caretakers for our planet. They make sure that the rules are followed to keep the environment safe and beautiful for everyone to enjoy!

Equity

Let's pretend you and your friends are building a treehouse together. You each bring different materials like wood, nails, and paint. Now, imagine one of your friends couldn't bring anything but still wanted to join in the fun. You might say, "That's okay, you can still be a part of the treehouse adventure! We'll give you a share of the treehouse for being part of the team."

In a company, "equity" is a bit like that share of the treehouse. It's a piece of ownership that someone has in the company, like owning a share of a big pizza. So, if a company is successful, everyone who has a piece of that "equity" gets to enjoy some of the rewards!

Escrow

Imagine you and your friend found a treasure map! But, you want to make sure it's a real map and not a fake one. So, you give the map to your mom and say, "Hold on to this until we find the treasure." Your mom keeps the map safe for you. That way, when you find the real treasure, you can all celebrate together!

In the business world, "escrow" is a bit like that. When people want to make sure something valuable, like money or important documents, are kept safe until a deal is completed, they put it in a special account with someone trusted, like a referee in a game. This person doesn't pick sides, they just make sure everything is fair and square!

Estate Planning and Probate Law Firms

Let's imagine you have a super cool treehouse that you love a lot. You want to make sure it stays awesome even if something happens to you. So, you make a plan that says if anything happens, your little brother or sister will be in charge of the treehouse. It's like giving them a treasure map with all the instructions!

Estate planning is kind of like that. It's when grown-ups make a plan for all the things they own, like their house, toys, and money. They decide who will take care of everything if they can't. And when they pass away (which is a natural part of life), the plan helps make sure everything goes to the right people, just like your treehouse going to your little brother or sister.

Ethical Dilemma

Pretend you're playing a game with your friends, and there's a rule that says no peeking. But then, you accidentally see the answer. Now you're stuck in a bit of a pickle, right? You have a choice to make: do you tell your friends you saw the answer, or do you keep it a secret and pretend you didn't?

An ethical dilemma is like being in a situation where you have to decide between two choices, and both choices have good and bad parts. It's like the peeking situation - telling the truth is good because it's honest, but it might also make your friends a little upset. Keeping it a secret might keep your friends happy, but it's not exactly honest.

So, an ethical dilemma is like being in a spot where you have to think really hard about what's the right thing to do, even when both choices have some good and not-so-good parts. It's like trying to decide in a tricky game!

Ethics

Imagine you and your friends are playing a game. There's a rule that says everyone has to take turns, and no one should skip their turn. Imagine one of your friends really, really wants to win, so they try to skip their turn secretly. That wouldn't be fair, right?

Ethics is like the rules of a game, but for life and work. It's about doing what's fair and right, even when no one is watching. It's about being honest, kind, and treating everyone with respect. So, just like you wouldn't want your friend to cheat in a game, in the real world, we try to follow good ethics to make sure everyone gets a fair chance to succeed.

Ethics and Compliance

Imagine you and your friends are playing a big game together. But this isn't just any game, it's a super special game with extra rules to make sure everyone plays fairly.

Now, imagine there's a judge watching to make sure everyone follows those rules. This judge makes sure nobody cheats or tries to do things that aren't allowed. They're like the referee in a sports match, making sure everything is fair and square.

In a company, ethics and compliance are a bit like those extra rules and the judge. They make sure everyone plays by fair and honest guidelines. It's like having a special team that keeps an eye on things to make sure everything is done the right way. This way, everyone has a fair chance to succeed, and the company can be proud of the way they do business.

Exit Strategy

Pretend you and your friends are building an amazing fort together. You've got walls made of cushions, a roof made of blankets, and a secret entrance made of stuffed animals. It's the coolest fort ever!

Now, let's say it's getting late, and everyone needs to go home. You can't leave the fort standing in the middle of the room, right? So, you need a plan. Your exit strategy might be to carefully take the fort down, making sure to remember how to build it again next time.

In the world of companies, an exit strategy is kind of like that plan for taking down the fort. It's a smart plan for how the owners or leaders of a company can leave when the time is right. Maybe they sell the company to someone else or they decide to go in a different direction. Just like with the fort, having a good exit strategy helps everything go smoothly.

Expert (vs. Professional)

Let's pretend we're in a big kitchen where they make delicious meals.

An "Expert" chef is like a super-duper, top-level chef. They've been cooking for a long, long time, and they can make all kinds of amazing dishes. It's like they're the masters of the kitchen, knowing all the secret recipes.

Now, a "Professional" chef is still really good, but they might be a bit newer to the kitchen. They've studied and trained a lot, and they can make really tasty food too. They're like the skilled chefs you see in good restaurants.

So, an "Expert" is like the super chef with lots and lots of experience, while a "Professional" is like a really good chef who's on their way to becoming an expert. They both make yummy food, but one has been cooking for a super long time!

In a nutshell, an Expert is skilled at work, while a Professional gets paid for their work.

Fair Market Value

Let's imagine you have a super rare and really awesome trading card. Now, imagine that there's a big event where lots of people who love trading cards are gathered. They all want to trade cards with each other.

Now, imagine a friend comes up to you and says, "Hey, I really want that trading card of yours. What do you think is a fair deal?" They're asking what you believe is a good and fair trade for your card.

Fair market value is a bit like that. It's the price that most people agree is fair for something when they're buying or selling it. Just like when you're trading cards, you want to make sure the deal feels right for everyone.

Family Law Firms

Let's imagine a big game of tag on the playground. In this game, there are special rules for when you're playing with family members. It's like having a mini-game within the big game.

Now, think of Family Law Firms like the referees of this special tag game. They're the ones who know all the special rules for families. If there's a disagreement or someone needs help with family stuff, they step in and make sure everything is fair and everyone is treated right, just like how the referees make sure everyone plays by the rules in the tag game!

Fast Track

Imagine you're in a big race with your friends. There's a regular track that goes all the way around, but there's also a special shortcut, like a secret passage. This secret passage is called the "fast track." If you take it, you can get to the finish line much quicker than if you stayed on the regular track. In the grown-up world, when someone talks about the "fast track," they mean finding a quicker and more efficient way to get things done, just like taking that shortcut in the race!

Fiduciary

Let's imagine you have a super responsible friend, let's call them Aris. Now, Aris is like your personal superhero for making sure things are done just right. They're like the guardian of a super secret treasure chest. They always make sure the treasure stays safe and is used wisely. That's kind of like what a "fiduciary" does in the grown-up world.

A fiduciary is someone who takes care of really important stuff for other people, like their money or valuable things. They have a big responsibility to make sure everything is handled in the best way possible, just like how Aris watches over that precious treasure. They're like a super trustworthy friend who always has your back!

Fiduciary Duty

Imagine you're the captain of a pirate ship. Your crew looks up to you and trusts you to make the best decisions for everyone on board. You have a special duty to take care of your crew's treasures, making sure they're kept safe and used wisely.

In a company, there are leaders too, like the captain of a ship. They're responsible for making important decisions that affect everyone involved. One of their most important jobs is to take care of the company's resources and make sure they're used in the best way for everyone. This special duty is called a fiduciary duty. It's a bit like being the trusted captain, making sure everything runs smoothly and fairly for everyone on the team.

Financial Forecasting

Alright, let's play a game called "Weather Wizard"! Imagine you're in charge of predicting the weather for a whole week in your town. You look at the sky, check the clouds, and maybe even use a special tool to help you make your predictions.

In a company, they have their own kind of wizardry called "Financial Forecasting." It's like being a Weather Wizard, but instead of predicting the weather, you're predicting how well the company will do financially in the future. You look at numbers, trends, and maybe even use special tools to make your predictions. It helps the company plan ahead and make smart decisions about money, a bit like how your weather predictions help people plan their week!

Financial Statement

Imagine you have a magical map that shows you all the treasures hidden in different parts of a big island. This map not only tells you where the treasures are, but also how much gold and jewels they hold.

In the world of companies, they have something similar called "Financial Statements." These are like special maps that show all the money a company has, where it comes from, and where it's going. Just like our magical map helps us plan treasure hunts, these statements help the company make smart decisions about their money. They have different sections like 'Income' to show how much money they're making, and 'Expenses' to show where they're spending it. It's like a magical guidebook for a company's money adventures!

Fixed Costs

Think of fixed costs like the rent on your clubhouse. Every month, you and your friends pay the same amount to use the space. It doesn't matter if you have a lot of meetings or just a few, the rent stays the same.

In business, fixed costs are a bit like the rent for a company. They're the expenses that stay the same no matter how much they produce or sell. Things like rent for the office, insurance, and salaries for certain staff members are considered fixed costs. Just like your clubhouse rent, these costs are consistent month after month.

Fixed-Rate Mortgage

Imagine you have a special toy chest at home where you keep all your favorite toys. Now, let's say you have a deal with your parents. Every week, you can borrow a toy from the chest and play with it as much as you want. But here's the cool part: the number of toys you can take each week and how long you can keep them is always the same. So, if you borrow two toys, you get to keep them for two weeks, and if you borrow three, you get to keep them for three weeks.

A Fixed-Rate Mortgage is kind of like that toy deal, but for grown-ups and houses. When they borrow money from the bank to buy a house, they agree to pay it back a little bit at a time, and the amount they pay and how long they have to pay it stays the same, just like in our toy deal. It helps them plan their budget and know exactly what to expect. Cool, right?

Foreclosure

Let's imagine you have a really cool treehouse. It's your favorite place to play and have adventures. Now, imagine if you couldn't take care of it for a really long time. You didn't fix the broken steps, and you didn't patch up the holes in the roof.

One day, if things get really bad, your parents might say, "We need to take the treehouse back because we can't let it get all run-down." That's a bit like what happens with foreclosure. When grown-ups buy a house but can't keep up with paying for it, the bank might say, "We need to take the house back because it's not being taken care of." They do this so they can find someone else who can take care of it properly.

Foreign Corporation

Imagine you have a clubhouse with a secret password that only your closest friends know. Now, think about a friend from another neighborhood who wants to join your club. They decide to build their own clubhouse, but it's in their own neighborhood, not yours. That's a bit like how a foreign corporation is a company from a different country. They have their own "clubhouse" where they do their business. They might even have their own special rules and ways of doing things. They're like your friends from another neighborhood, but in the world of grown-up businesses!

Franchise

Let's pretend you have a super cool recipe for making the most amazing cookies ever. Now, imagine you meet a friend who loves your cookies and wants to make them too, but they don't know the secret recipe. So, you decide to share your recipe with them and let them sell the cookies in their own special cookie shop. They use your recipe, but they run their own shop.

That's a bit like a franchise! It's when a big company (like a famous cookie recipe company) lets other people (your friend) use their special way of doing things and sell their products in their own stores. So, even though it's not your store, it's still using your amazing cookie recipe!

Franchise Agreement

Imagine you have a really cool recipe for making special cookies, and you want to share it with your friends. But you can't be everywhere to make these cookies, so you decide to let your friends use your recipe and make their own.

You create some rules to make sure they make the cookies just right. In return, they give you a little bit of the money they make selling the cookies. That's a bit like a franchise agreement in business.

In a company, a franchise agreement is a bit like your cookie recipe. The company has a successful way of doing things, and they let other people use it (like opening a store with their name and way of doing things). But there are rules to follow to make sure everything is just right. In return, the company gets a share of the money the new store makes. It's a way for the company to grow and share their success with others!

Functional Organization

Let's imagine your school is getting ready for a big event like a talent show. There are different groups of people in charge of different things. One group is responsible for picking the acts, another for setting up the stage, and another for handling the tickets.

Each group has a specific job, and they work really well because they focus on what they're best at. This is a bit like a "Functional Organization" in a company. Different teams focus on their own special jobs, like the talent show groups, so everything comes together smoothly!

* * *

We would love to hear from **all of you** who supported this book!

Your **positive review** on *Amazon* would not only mean a lot to us, but it would also help other readers discover the book and embark on their own culinary adventure.

All it takes is just a minute to make a difference!

5

G, H, I, J, K, L, M - Corporate Terms

Game Changer

Imagine you're playing a board game with your friends, and it's really close. But then, someone pulls out a special card that completely changes the rules of the game! Suddenly, everything is different, and it gives them a big advantage. That special card is like a "game changer." In the grown-up world, when people talk about a "game changer," they mean something that comes along and totally changes how things are done, just like that special card in your game!

Game Plan

Imagine you're going on a treasure hunt with a map. The map shows you where the hidden treasure is, but it also has some tricky spots and obstacles you'll have to navigate around. Your "game plan" is like looking at the map and figuring out the best way to get to the treasure without getting stuck or lost. In the grown-up world, a "game plan" is like a special strategy or set of steps people come up with to reach their goals, just like how you plan your route to find the treasure!

General Ledger

Think of the general ledger like a big, special notebook that keeps track of all the money coming in and going out of your club. Every time someone gives money for snacks or you spend it on decorations, you write it down in this special notebook. This way, you always know how much money you have and where it's going.

In business, the general ledger is a bit like that special notebook. It's where all the money stuff is written down. When a company gets money from selling things or spends money on supplies, they write it in the general ledger. This helps them keep track of how much money they have and where it's being used. It's like the super organized financial memory of the company!

General Practice Law Firms

Imagine you're a super detective, like the ones in your favorite mystery books. You're not just good at solving one type of mystery, like finding lost pets or figuring out puzzles. No, you're awesome at solving all sorts of mysteries! Missing items, tricky riddles, and even helping people who need legal advice. You're like a mystery-solving expert in many different areas.

Well, that's kind of what a General Practice Law Firm is like. Instead of just focusing on one type of law, like only helping with car accidents or just working on wills, they're like the super detectives of the legal world. They can handle all sorts of different legal matters, just like you with all those different kinds of mysteries!

Going Forward

Going forward is like riding a bike. When you're on a bike, you're not looking behind you, you're looking ahead to see where you're going. In the same way, when people talk about "going forward" in a corporate setting, they're thinking about the future and planning what they want to do next, just like you do when you're riding your bike and looking ahead to see where you want to go!

Golden Parachute

Let's imagine you and your friends are playing a game where you're all superheroes. You each have a special power, like flying or super strength. Now, let's say the game is about to end, and someone gives you a special gift for being an awesome superhero. This gift is like a "Golden Parachute."

It's not an actual parachute, but it's something really special that you get when the game ends. It's like a big, shiny reward for being a top-notch superhero. In the world of grown-ups and companies, a "Golden Parachute" is a special kind of reward that top executives might get when they leave a company, like getting a big bonus or special benefits. It's like a way of saying "Thanks for being an amazing superhero in our company!"

Government Agency

Let's pretend you're playing in a big playground with lots of different areas. You've got the swings, the slides, the climbing frames, and even a little sports area. Each of these play areas has different rules and helpers.

Now, imagine if there were special grown-ups whose job was to make sure everything in the playground runs smoothly. They might check if the swings are safe, or help if someone gets a little scrape. They're like the 'playground police'! These grown-ups are a bit like a Government Agency. They look after different parts of our community, like parks, roads, and even things like health and safety rules, to make sure everything is fair and safe for everyone.

Government Law Firms

Let's picture a big game of soccer. You've got two teams, one wearing blue jerseys and the other in red. Each team has its own coach who tells them the rules and helps them play their best.

Now, imagine if there were special coaches whose job was to make sure all the teams in the league play fairly. They might check if everyone's following the rules and help if there's a disagreement. These special coaches are a bit like Government Law Firms. They make sure everyone is playing by the rules in the 'game' of following laws in our community.

Gross Domestic Product (GDP)

Imagine your friend has a big garden where they grow all sorts of fruits and vegetables. They pick all the ripe fruits and veggies and count them up to see how much they've grown. That's a bit like calculating Gross Domestic Product (GDP) for a country.

In a country, GDP is like counting up all the fruits and veggies that have been grown, but instead of fruits and veggies, it's about all the goods and services that the country produces. It helps us understand how much the country is 'growing' economically. So, just like your friend counts up their harvest, we count up all the things a country makes to see how well it's doing economically!

Gross Margin

Think of gross margin like a lemonade stand. You and your friends sell cups of lemonade, and you have to buy lemons, sugar, and cups to make it. Let's say you sell each cup for a dollar. After you subtract the cost of the lemons, sugar, and cups, you have some money left over. That extra money is like your gross margin.

In business, gross margin is a bit like the extra money you have after selling lemonade. It's what's left after you subtract the cost of making or buying the things you're selling. It's an important number because it helps you understand how much profit you're making before you take out all the other expenses.

Gross Profit Margin

Imagine you're running a lemonade stand. You have your table, cups, lemons, and sugar. You sell each cup of lemonade for a certain price. Now, let's say you add up all the money you made and subtract the cost of the lemons, sugar, and cups. The money left over is your "Gross Profit."

The Gross Profit Margin is like looking at how much money you have left after you take away the costs of making the lemonade. It helps you see how well you're doing at making a profit. So, if you're making a lot more money than you're spending on ingredients, that's a good sign! It means your Gross

Profit Margin is high, and your lemonade stand is doing great!

Growth Hacking

Let's imagine you have a lemonade stand. You start by selling lemonade to your neighbors, and that's going well. But one day, you decide to put up a sign in your front yard with a big arrow that points to your lemonade stand. Suddenly, more people start coming to buy your lemonade!

Growth hacking in the business world is a bit like that. It's when a company tries creative and sometimes unconventional strategies to make their business grow really fast. They might use things like social media, special promotions, or new ideas to get a lot more customers quickly, just like your sign brought in more lemonade customers. So, growth hacking is all about finding clever ways to make a business grow and succeed!

Healthcare Law Firms

Let's pretend we have a big team of doctors and nurses, like a soccer team, but they're not playing a game. Instead, they're taking care of people when they're sick or hurt.

Now, imagine if there were special coaches who helped the doctors and nurses understand all the rules and make sure everyone gets the right care. These special coaches are a bit like Healthcare Law Firms. They make sure everyone in the 'healthcare game' is doing things the right way and looking out for patients.

Hedge Fund

Imagine you have a big box of different kinds of candies. Some candies are really popular and everyone wants them, while others are not as well-known. Now, you have a friend who knows a lot about candies and can predict which ones will become really popular in the future.

So, your friend says, 'Let's put some money together, and I'll buy more of the candies I think will be really popular in the future.' If your friend is right, you all make some extra money. But if not, you might not make as much.

In the world of finance, a hedge fund is a bit like that candy strategy. It's a group of people who pool their money together and have someone who's really good at picking investments. They try to make more money by investing in things they believe will become very valuable in the future. It's a bit like a candy gamble, but with money and investments!

Home Inspection

Let's imagine you're a detective in a mystery story. You've been given the important job of checking a house for any hidden clues or secrets. You're like a super-sleuth making sure everything is safe and sound. That's a bit like what a Home Inspection is in the world of houses. It's when experts go through a house with a fine-tooth comb, looking for any little mysteries or problems that need solving before someone can move in.

Homeowner's Association (HOA)

Let's imagine you and your friends have a special clubhouse where you all play and have fun. To keep everything running smoothly, you make some rules. These rules help everyone know how to share the space and keep it nice for everyone. A Homeowner's Association, or HOA, is a bit like having these rules for a big group of neighbors who all live in the same area. They work together to make sure everything stays tidy, safe, and friendly for everyone who lives there. It's like having a big clubhouse agreement for a whole bunch of houses!

Horizontal Integration

Let's pretend you have a bunch of different fruit trees in your garden. You've got apple trees, orange trees, and even some peach trees. Each tree gives you a different type of fruit.

Now, one day, you have an idea. What if you could combine all these fruits and make a delicious mixed fruit salad? So, you start picking apples, oranges, and peaches and mix them all together.

In the world of companies, when one company joins forces with another that's in a similar line of business, like if a company that makes bicycles joins up with a company that makes skateboards, that's a bit like making a mixed fruit salad in the business world. This joining together is called "Horizontal Integration." Just like mixing fruits makes a tasty salad, companies merging can sometimes make something even better together!

Human Resources

Alright, let's imagine your school is like a big puzzle. Each student, teacher, and staff member is a different piece of the puzzle. Now, who's responsible for making sure all the puzzle pieces fit together nicely and everyone is in the right place doing the right things? That's the job of the puzzle master!

In a company, the puzzle master is called Human Resources, or HR for short. They're like the friendly wizards who help find the right people for the right jobs, make sure everyone is happy and comfortable, and even organize fun activities for everyone to enjoy. They're like the magic glue that keeps the whole company puzzle together!

Human Resources Development (HRD)

Think of Human Resources Development (HRD) like a garden that your parents take care of. They plant seeds, water the plants, and make sure they get enough sun. They do all these things so that the garden can grow and be healthy.

In a company, HRD is a bit like taking care of the people who work there. They make sure everyone has the right training, tools, and support to do their jobs well. It's like helping each person in the company grow and be the best they can be, just like taking care of the plants in a garden. When everyone is doing their best, the company can grow and be successful too!

Ideation

Let's imagine you're an inventor. You have a special room filled with all sorts of cool gadgets, paints, and craft supplies. When you want to come up with new inventions, you go into this room and start putting things together, trying out different combinations, and experimenting.

Ideation in the business world is a bit like your inventor's room. It's the process of coming up with lots of different ideas for new products, services, or solutions. Just like you try out different materials and tools in your room, businesses brainstorm and experiment with various concepts to see which ones might turn into something really amazing! So, ideation is all about using your imagination to create something new and exciting.

Immigration Law Firms

Imagine you have a big puzzle with pieces from all over the world. Each piece represents a person who wants to come and live in your town. But not every puzzle piece fits perfectly, some need a little help to find their right spot. Immigration Law Firms are like the experts who know all the special tricks for helping these puzzle pieces (people) find their perfect spot in the community. They make sure everyone follows the rules and helps them on their journey to becoming a part of the big picture.

Income Statement

Think of an income statement like a scorecard for a soccer game. It tells you how many goals your team scored and how many the other team scored. It helps you see who's winning and by how much.

In business, an income statement is a bit like a scorecard, but for money. It shows how much money the company made (which is like the goals they scored) and how much they spent (which is like the goals the other team scored). This way, everyone can see how well the company is doing financially. Just like in a soccer game, it helps you understand who's winning in the world of business!

Initial Coin Offering (ICO)

Imagine you and your friends have a really cool idea for a new game. You all pitch in some money to make it happen, and in return, you get special tokens that let you be the first ones to play the game when it's ready.

In the world of business, an Initial Coin Offering (ICO) is a bit like that game idea. A company has a new and exciting project, and they want to make it happen. They ask people to invest in it, and in return, they get special digital tokens. These tokens can sometimes be used to access or use the new thing the company is creating, like playing a game. It's a way for the company to get support and for people to be part of something new and exciting!

Initial Exchange Offering (IEO)

Imagine you're at a big playground with lots of rides and games. There's a special ride that's brand new and everyone is really excited to try it. To get on, you need a special ticket that's only available for a short time.

In the world of business, an Initial Exchange Offering (IEO) is a bit like that special ride. A company has a new project they're really excited about, and they're offering special 'tickets' (like digital tokens) for people to get involved.

These tokens might give you special access or benefits related to the project, just like the special ticket lets you enjoy the new ride at the playground. It's a way for people to be part of something exciting from the very start!

Initial Public Offering (IPO)

Imagine you and your friends love making delicious lemonade. Your lemonade stand is so popular that you decide to open a big lemonade stand with lots of stands all over the city. But to make it happen, you need more money.

So, you tell your friends, 'Let's all chip in some money, and in return, we'll all be owners of the big lemonade stand company.' You also decide to invite other people in the neighborhood to join in, and they can be owners too by buying a special share.

In the business world, an Initial Public Offering (IPO) is a bit like that big lemonade stand idea. A company that's been doing really well decides to let regular people become owners by buying shares. It's like inviting everyone in the neighborhood to be a part of your lemonade stand adventure. It helps the company get the money they need to grow, and lots of people get to be a part of it!

Innovation

Let's say you have a big box of building blocks, and you've been building awesome towers and castles. But one day, you decide to create something completely new, something no one has ever seen before! So, you start combining the blocks in a whole new way, using your creativity and imagination.

In a company, when they come up with brand new ideas or ways of doing things that nobody else has thought of before, that's called innovation. It's like inventing a new game to play with your building blocks. It's what makes a company stand out and do really amazing things!

Insider Trading

Picture a big game of hide and seek. Imagine you're playing with a group of friends, and one friend sneaks a peek to see where everyone else is hiding. They have an unfair advantage, right? It wouldn't be a fair game anymore.

Well, in the world of companies and stocks, there's a rule called "insider trading." It's like a big game where everyone should have the same information. If someone inside the company, like an employee or a big boss, sneaks a peek at secret information about the company, and then uses that information to make decisions about buying or selling stocks, it's not fair to the other players in the game. It's against the rules because it gives them an unfair advantage.

So, insider trading is like peeking during hide and seek – it's not fair, and it's not allowed in the world of business!

Intellectual Property

Imagine you create an amazing, one-of-a-kind comic book with your own characters and stories. You're really proud of it! To make sure no one copies your awesome ideas, you put a special invisible shield around it. This shield is super strong, and it makes sure that only you and the people you choose can use or copy your comic book.

In the world of business, intellectual property is a bit like that invisible shield. It's like a superpower that protects things like your special ideas, inventions, or even songs and stories. It makes sure that the person who came up with the cool stuff gets to decide how it's used. Just like you with your amazing comic book!

Intellectual Property Law Firms

Let's imagine you're a super creative artist, and you've made up a brand new game all on your own. It's got cool characters, awesome rules, and is super fun to play. Now, you want to make sure no one else copies your game and tries to say it's theirs. That's where Intellectual Property Law Firms come in. They're like the guardians of your game, making sure nobody takes credit for your amazing creation. They use special rules and laws to keep your game safe, just like a superhero protecting a city!

Intellectual Property Rights (IPR)

Let's pretend you're a super talented artist. You create amazing drawings, paintings, and crafts. Now, imagine if someone tried to copy your artwork and say it was theirs! That wouldn't be fair, right?

Well, in the business world, there are special rules called Intellectual Property Rights (IPR). It's like a superhero cape that protects your ideas and creations. These rights say, "Hey, this is mine! You can't just take it without asking." It's important because it encourages people to come up with new and awesome things, knowing they'll be rewarded and recognized for their hard work and creativity. So, IPR is like a shield that keeps your brilliant ideas safe and sound!

International Law Firms

Let's say you have a bunch of friends who live in different parts of the world. Sometimes, you might have disagreements or need to make special rules when you all play games together. That's where International Law Firms come in. They're like the wise, fair referees of the world. They help everyone understand the rules and make sure things are fair for everyone, no matter where they're from. So, it's like having a referee that knows how to play games with people from all over the planet!

Intrapreneurship

Alright, let's go on an adventure! Imagine you're in a big castle. But instead of being a knight or a princess, you're like a creative inventor. You look around and see all these rooms filled with tools and materials. There's wood, paint, gears, and all sorts of interesting stuff.

Now, here's the cool part: you don't have to wait for someone to tell you what to make. You can come up with your own amazing ideas and start building them! Maybe you want to create a magical flying machine or a new kind of toy that's never been seen before. That's intrapreneurship!

In a big company, sometimes there are special people who get to do this. They're like castle inventors. They have the freedom to come up with new and exciting things, even if they don't own the castle themselves. They use the company's tools and resources to bring their awesome ideas to life. It's like being an inventor right in the heart of the castle!

Inventory Turnover

Imagine you have a big box of crayons, all different colors. You use these crayons to create beautiful drawings. Now, think about how quickly you can use up all the crayons and need to get new ones. If you use up the crayons very fast and need to buy new ones often, that's like a store with a high "Inventory Turnover."

On the other hand, if you take a long time to use up your crayons and rarely need to buy new ones, that's like a store with a low "Inventory Turnover." It's a bit like when you finish your snacks quickly, and your mom has to buy more from the store sooner, or when they last a long time, and she doesn't need to shop as often. Inventory turnover helps businesses figure out how fast they sell their stuff and how often they need to restock their shelves.

Joint Venture (JV)

Imagine you and your friend both love baking cookies. One day, you decide to team up and make a special kind of cookie together. You bring your favorite ingredients, and your friend brings theirs. You work together in the kitchen, sharing ideas and helping each other out. When the cookies are ready, you both get to enjoy the delicious treat.

This teamwork in making cookies is a bit like a "Joint Venture" in the business world. It's when two companies come together to work on a special project or create something new. They bring their strengths and resources to the table and share in the success of the project, just like you and your friend did with the cookies.

Joint Venture Agreement

Let's say you and your best friend both love building amazing treehouses. One day, you decide to team up and build the most incredible treehouse ever. You each bring your own special tools and ideas to the project. You sit down and make a list of all the things you promise to do, like who will bring which tools and who will do certain tasks.

This list you make is like a "Joint Venture Agreement" in the business world. It's like a special promise between two companies when they decide to work together on a big project. They write down all the important details about what each company will do, just like you and your friend wrote down your promises for building the awesome treehouse. This way, everyone knows what to expect, and the project can run smoothly.

Just-in-Time (JIT)

Let's pretend you're a superhero and you have a special power. This power lets you summon exactly the right tools and gadgets you need, right when you need them, just in the nick of time to save the day! You don't carry around a whole bunch of stuff you might not use. You only bring out what you need, exactly when you need it.

In the business world, there's something called "Just-in-Time" or JIT for short. It's like being a superhero for companies. Instead of storing a ton of stuff they might not need right away, they get things delivered right when they need them. This helps companies save space, money, and work really efficiently. It's like magic for businesses!

Kanban

Let's imagine you're a chef in a really busy kitchen. You've got a big menu with lots of different dishes to make. But you can't make everything at once, right? That would be really chaotic! So, you have a board where you list out all the dishes you need to make. When you finish one, you take it off the board and start on the next.

In a company, especially ones that make things, they use something called Kanban. It's like the chef's board, but for tasks or projects. They have a visual board where they list out all the tasks that need to be done. When one task is finished, they move it off the board and start on the next one. This helps everyone stay organized and make sure everything gets done in the right order!

Key Account Management (KAM)

Alright, let's imagine you're a super organized kid running a lemonade stand. You've got a bunch of customers, but there are a few really special ones who always buy a lot of lemonade. You know them by name, and you even have a little notebook where you keep track of what they like. When they come by, you make sure they get the best service and maybe even offer them a little extra, like a free cookie.

In a big company, they have something called Key Account Management, which is kind of like your lemonade stand. They have some really important customers that buy a lot, and they want to make sure those customers are super happy. They have special teams who take care of these special customers, just like you take special care of your top lemonade buyers!

Key Performance Indicators (KPIs)

Imagine you're playing a video game where you're a superhero saving a city. To know how well you're doing, you have a special screen that shows you things like how many bad guys you've caught, how many buildings you've rescued, and how fast you're moving. These things help you see if you're doing a great job or if you need to step up your game.

Well, in a big company, they have something similar called Key Performance Indicators, or KPIs. Instead of fighting bad guys, they're measuring things like how many products they sell, how satisfied their customers are, and how efficiently they're working. It's like a special dashboard that helps them know if they're doing a super job in running their business!

Key Performance Objectives (KPOs)

Imagine you're a student in a school. Your teacher gives you a special list of things they want you to achieve by the end of the year. It might be things like getting good grades, doing a cool science project, and being a helpful classmate.

In a big company, they have something similar called Key Performance Objectives, or KPOs. It's like a special list of important goals they want to achieve. For them, it might be selling a certain number of products, making sure their customers are super happy, and always coming up with new and exciting ideas. These objectives help them stay on track and do a great job in their business, just like your goals help you do your best in school!

Key Result Areas (KRAs)

Imagine you're a superhero with a special mission to protect your city. But being a superhero isn't just about saving people from danger. It's also about making sure the city stays clean, the parks are nice, and everyone is happy and safe.

In a big company, they have something similar called Key Result Areas, or KRAs. It's like each person in the company has their own special mission to help the company succeed. For some, it might be making sure the customers are really happy, for others, it could be creating awesome new products. Just like each superhero has their own role in keeping the city awesome, each person in the company has a special job to make the company successful!

Key Success Factors (KSFs)

Let's imagine you're a soccer player. You really want to win games, right? So, there are certain things you need to do to be successful on the field. You need to practice your dribbling, passing, and shooting skills. You also need to be a good team player, listen to your coach, and stay in good shape. These are your Key Success Factors for being a great soccer player.

In the corporate world, companies also have Key Success Factors, or KSFs. These are like the important skills and strategies a company needs to be successful. It could be things like making high-quality products, giving excellent customer service, or finding new and exciting ways to do business. Just like you have to work on your skills to be a top-notch soccer player, a company has to focus on its Key Success Factors to be a successful business!

Known-Knowns/Known-Unknowns/Unknown-Knowns/Unknown-Unknowns

Alright, let's dive into the world of mystery books! Imagine you have a big stack of books, but some of them you know really well because you've read them before. These are like your "Known-Knowns." You know all the characters, the plot twists, and how it all ends. It's like reading your favorite story for the tenth time.

Then there are books that you've heard about, but you haven't read them yet. You know they exist, but you're not sure what happens in them. These are like your "Known-Unknowns." You know they're out there, but the details are still a bit of a mystery.

Now, imagine finding a secret diary hidden under your bed. You didn't even know it was there! This is like an "Unknown-Known." It was right there, but you didn't realize it until now.

And finally, there might be books in the library that you've never even heard of. They're a complete surprise! These are like your "Unknown-Unknowns." You have no idea what's inside until you open them up.

In the business world, sometimes we have information that we know really well (Known-Knowns), some things we've heard about but don't fully understand yet (Known-Unknowns), sometimes we discover information that we didn't realize we had (Unknown-Knowns), and there are also things that are completely new and surprising to us (Unknown-Unknowns). It's a bit like exploring a library of mysteries!

Landlord

Let's imagine you have a clubhouse in your backyard that you built with your own toys and furniture. You're in charge of it, and you decide who gets to come in to play. Now, imagine if someone else in your family, like your big brother or sister, was the boss of the clubhouse. They would be like the landlord. They make sure everything is in good shape, and they might ask you for some special things, like helping to clean up after a big playtime. They're like the caretaker of the clubhouse!

Lean Manufacturing

Let's pretend you have a big box of colorful crayons. When you want to make a beautiful drawing, you don't use all the crayons at once, right? That would be messy and confusing! Instead, you pick the colors you need and arrange them neatly on the table. This way, you can create your masterpiece with just the right tools.

In a factory, when they make things like toys or cars, they also want to be organized and use only what they need. Lean Manufacturing is a bit like your organized crayons. It's a way for factories to be super efficient. They figure out exactly what they need, use the right machines, and make things quickly and neatly, just like you do when you're creating your artwork!

Lean Six Sigma

Let's imagine you're building an amazing tower out of building blocks. You want it to be tall, strong, and perfect.

Lean Six Sigma is like having a special set of tools and a plan to build your tower. The "Lean" part helps you use only the blocks you really need, so you don't waste any. It's like picking out just the right colors and shapes for your tower.

The "Six Sigma" part is like having a super-duper quality checker. It makes sure every block is in the right place and everything fits together perfectly, just like a puzzle.

So, with Lean Six Sigma, you can build the most amazing, super tall tower using the least amount of blocks, and it will be super sturdy and perfect!

Lease

Let's imagine you have a super cool treehouse in your backyard. But instead of owning it forever, you let your friend use it for a certain amount of time. It's like you're giving them a special permission slip to play in your awesome treehouse for a few months. That special permission slip is called a lease! It's like a contract that says, "You can use my treehouse, but only for this amount of time, and you have to take care of it really well." Cool, right?

Letter of Agreement (LOA)

Let's imagine you and your friend want to do a big project together, like building a treehouse. But you need to agree on some important things, like who will do what, what materials you'll use, and how you'll share the treehouse.

A Letter of Agreement is like a special note where you write down all these important details. It's like making a list of rules and plans so everyone knows what to expect. It's a bit like making a "treehouse plan" that you and your friend both sign, so you're both on the same page about the project!

Letter of Intent (LOI)

Let's imagine you really, really want to have a sleepover at your friend's house. You're super excited about it! So, before you ask your parents, you might write a special note to your friend. In this note, you'd say something like, "I really, really, REALLY want to have a sleepover at your house! If it's okay with your parents, I promise to be super well-behaved and we'll have a blast!"

A Letter of Intent (LOI) is kind of like that special note. It's a letter that says, "Hey, I'm really interested in doing something with you, and if everything works out, I'm all in and super excited about it!" It's a way to show you're really keen on doing something together.

Leverage

Let's imagine you're on a seesaw at the playground. When you're by yourself, it's sometimes a bit tricky to go up and down because you have to use all your strength. But, if you have a friend on the other side, it's much easier! You can go up and down smoothly because you're using the seesaw's "help" to move.

In the business world, "leverage" is a bit like having a friend on the other side of the seesaw. It means using something you already have (like money, knowledge, or resources) to help you do more or go further. Just like the seesaw, it makes things easier and more effective!

Leveraged Buyout (LBO)

Pretend you're in a game where you get to build and run your own little town. You've got a bunch of toy houses, shops, and even a little bank where you keep all your pretend money.

Now, let's say you really want to make your town even cooler. You have a great idea to add a big, awesome amusement park right in the middle. The thing is, building an amusement park costs a lot of money, and you don't have quite enough in your pretend bank.

So, you decide to do something super smart. You talk to your friends and ask if they want to join in on this amazing amusement park project. They think it's a fantastic idea and are happy to help. They each chip in some of their pretend money, and together, you have enough to build the amusement park!

That's kind of like what happens in a leveraged buyout (LBO). A bunch of grown-ups, like business wizards, team up and pool their money to buy a company. They believe in the company's potential to grow and become even better, but they need to work together to make it happen. It's like turning your little town into the best town ever!

License

Imagine you have a super cool treehouse that you built all by yourself. It's your special place, and only you and your closest friends are allowed inside. Now, let's say you have a little brother or sister who really wants to come in and play. You might say, "I'll give you a special ticket to come in for a little while, but only if you promise to follow the rules and be really nice."

In the business world, a "license" is a bit like that special ticket. When a company gives someone a license, they're saying, "You can use our special thing, but only if you promise to follow the rules we've set." It's a way of sharing or letting others use something valuable for a specific purpose.

Licensed (vs. Certified)

Alright, imagine you have a collection of awesome adventure gear. Some of these items are "Certified" by a super wise adventurer. This means they've carefully checked each piece and said, "Yes, these are the best and safest tools for our quests."

Then, there are the "Licensed" tools. These are like the special items you let your close friends use. You say, "Alright, you can borrow these, but remember, handle them with care!"

So, when something is "Certified," it's like having the official seal of approval from the wisest adventurers. When something is "Licensed," it's like giving your pals permission to use it, but they have to be really careful. It's all about making sure everyone stays safe during their adventures!

Licensing Agreement

Let's imagine you have a really cool toy, like a super special rocket ship that you built. Now, imagine your friend wants to play with it too, but you want to make sure they take good care of it. So, you make a special agreement with your friend. You say, "Okay, you can play with it, but you have to promise to bring it back in the same condition." That's a bit like a "licensing agreement" in business.

In the business world, when a company has something special, like a really awesome invention or a popular character, they might let another company use it for a while. But, they have rules, just like you did with your rocket ship. They make an agreement that says, "You can use this, but you have to follow these rules and give it back in good shape." That's what we call a "licensing agreement." It's like sharing, but with special rules!

Lien

Let's imagine you have a super awesome collection of trading cards. Now, let's say you want to borrow some money from your friend, but you promise them that if you can't pay it back, they get to keep some of your favorite cards until you do. It's like putting a special sticker on those cards that says, "These cards are a guarantee for my friend until I can pay them back." That sticker is like a lien in the world of grown-ups! It's a way of saying, "I promise to give something valuable if I can't fulfill my promise." Cool, right?

Limited Liability Company (LLC)

Imagine you and your friends decide to build a cool treehouse together. You all put your toys and games inside it. Now, here's the fun part: you and your friends make a special rule that says, "If anything happens to the treehouse, we won't have to use our own toys to fix it. We'll only use the toys and games that are already inside the treehouse." So, even if something goes wrong, your personal toys are safe.

Well, that's a bit like how a Limited Liability Company, or LLC, works in the grown-up world. It's a group of people who start a business together and say, "If something goes wrong with the business, we won't have to use our personal stuff (like our cars or video games) to fix it. We'll only use the business's money and assets." This way, everyone's personal things are protected, just like your toys in the treehouse. Sounds cool, right?

Liquidation

Let's imagine you have a super-duper collection of trading cards. You love them, and they're really valuable! Now, you hear about a big swap meet happening in town. There, you can trade your cards for other cool stuff, like toys, games, or even more cards.

But wait, you've also noticed that some of your cards are getting a little worn out. They're not as shiny and awesome as they used to be. You decide it's time to say goodbye to these cards and get something cool in return.

So, you bring those cards to the swap meet. Some collectors are really excited about them, and they trade you some awesome new toys and games. You've turned your old cards into new treasures!

That's a bit like what happens in a corporate liquidation. When a company isn't doing so well, and it's time to close up shop, they sell off all their stuff— like buildings, machines, and sometimes even their products. They turn everything they have left into money, which they can use to pay off any debts or maybe even start something new and exciting!

Remember, just like you, companies can start fresh and find new adventures, too!

Liquidity Ratio

Let's imagine you have a big jar of marbles. Some of the marbles are really small, like tiny pebbles, and some are big, like shiny glass ones. Now, let's say you want to know how many big marbles you have compared to the small ones. To do that, you'd use a special measuring cup that can only hold a certain amount of marbles.

In the business world, companies have something similar. They want to know if they have enough of the important stuff, like money they can use easily, compared to the not-so-important stuff. This helps them figure out if they're in a good spot financially. That's kind of like a "liquidity ratio" for businesses. It's like making sure you have enough of the right marbles in your jar.

Listing Agent

Let's imagine you're the captain of a sports team. Your job is to pick the players who will be on your team and lead them to victory. You know each player's strengths and how they can contribute to winning the game.

In the business world, a Listing Agent is a bit like a team captain. They help people who want to sell their homes. The Listing Agent knows all the good things about the house and helps find the right buyers who would love to live there. They're like the leader who knows all the players' skills and chooses the best team for success, but instead of players, it's houses!

Low-Hanging Fruit

Imagine you're in a big orchard with lots of fruit trees. Some of the fruits are really high up in the branches, and you'd need a ladder to reach them. But then, there are some fruits that are so low, you can just pluck them with your hand, no ladder needed!

In a business, there are tasks and ideas that are a bit like those low-hanging fruits. They're the things that are easy to do, like quick wins, and they don't take a lot of effort. It's like picking the easy-to-reach fruit in the orchard. So, when people talk about "low-hanging fruit" in a company, they mean the easy tasks or ideas that can be done without too much trouble.

Maritime Law Firms

Let's set sail on an adventure! Imagine you and your friends decide to build a super cool treehouse in your backyard. You all agree on some important rules, like no roughhousing and taking turns using the cool telescope. These rules help make sure everyone has a great time and stays safe.

Maritime Law Firms are a bit like those rules, but for big ships and boats on the ocean. They help make sure everyone follows the right safety rules and agreements when they're out at sea. It's like having a set of important rules to make sure everyone has a fantastic time exploring the high seas!

Market Capitalization

Imagine you and your friends have a collection of trading cards. Each card has a special value. Now, think about the rarest and most sought-after cards in the collection. They're like the really special ones, right?

Market capitalization is a bit like that in the world of companies. It's a way of saying how special and valuable a company is. Instead of cards, we're talking about pieces of a company called "shares." The more valuable the shares, the bigger the market capitalization of the company. So, when people talk about market capitalization, they're trying to figure out just how special and valuable a company is in the big world of businesses.

Market Capitalization (Crypto)

Let's imagine a big treasure chest filled with different kinds of magical coins. Each coin represents a different kind of crypto coin. Now, some of these magical coins are very, very rare and special, just like the shiniest gemstones you've ever seen.

Market capitalization in the world of crypto is a bit like counting up how much all those magical coins are worth together. It helps people see which types of magical coins are the most sought-after and valuable in the world of digital treasures. So, when people talk about market capitalization in crypto, they're trying to figure out just how special and valuable each type of magical coin is in the big world of digital currencies.

Market Development

Let's imagine you have a cool new board game that you think is super fun to play. At first, it's just you and your friends who know about it. But you want more people to play and enjoy it, right?

Market development is like when you start telling other kids in your school about this amazing game. You might even invite them over to try it out. As more and more kids learn about the game and start playing, your game becomes super popular, and soon, it's the talk of the whole town! So, market development in business is all about getting more and more people interested in and using a new product or service. It's like spreading the word about your awesome game!

Market Expansion

Imagine you have this fantastic recipe for a delicious homemade pizza. You've been making it for your family, and they all love it. Now, you want to share it with even more people because it's just so tasty!

Market expansion is like deciding to set up a little pizza stand at a local fair. You bring all the ingredients and start making and selling your amazing pizza to everyone who passes by. Soon, word spreads about how yummy your pizza is, and more and more people line up to try it. You've gone from making pizza just for your family to serving it to a big crowd of happy pizza lovers!

In business, market expansion means finding new places or ways to sell a product or service so that even more people can enjoy it, just like when you shared your special pizza recipe with lots of new friends at the fair!

Market Penetration

Let's imagine you have a cool new game that you and your friends really enjoy playing. You want more of your friends to join in on the fun! So, you start inviting them over to play, and you even explain the rules to them so they can join in easily.

Market penetration in business is a bit like that. It's when a company already has a product, and they want to sell more of it to the same group of people or in the same area. They might do things like offering special deals, advertising more, or even improving the product to make sure more people want to buy it, just like you inviting more friends to play your awesome game!

Market Research

Let's imagine you really love playing a certain type of game, like a treasure hunt. Now, before you go on a big treasure hunt, you'd want to know where to look, right? You might ask your friends for tips, or even use a map to find the best spots.

Market research in business is a bit like that. Companies want to know where the best "treasures" (which in this case are customers who want to buy their products) are located. They do lots of investigations and surveys to figure out what people like and where they like to shop. This helps them know where to focus their efforts to find the most customers, just like you use a map to find the best places for your treasure hunt!

Market Segmentation

Let's pretend you have a big box of colorful crayons. Each crayon can draw a different type of picture. Some are great for drawing people, some for drawing animals, and others for drawing cool landscapes.

Market segmentation in business is a bit like that. Imagine a company makes toys. They want to know which toys are best for different groups of people. Just like you use specific crayons for different types of drawings, companies use market segmentation to figure out which products are best for different groups of customers. So, they can make sure everyone gets the toy they'd love the most!

Market Share

Imagine you and your friends are playing with a big box of delicious cookies. There are different types of cookies in the box, like chocolate chip, oatmeal, and peanut butter.

Now, let's say you and your friends each take some cookies from the box. If you have the most cookies out of everyone, you have the biggest "market share" of the cookies. It means you have more cookies than any of your friends.

In the business world, "market share" is similar. It's like saying one company has more customers or sells more products than the other companies in the same market. Just like you can have the most cookies among your friends, a company can have the most customers or sales in its industry.

Market Value

Let's go on an adventure in the land of trading cards! Imagine you have a really rare and awesome trading card, like a super cool dragon card. You and your friend both want to trade cards, but you have to figure out a fair exchange. You look at how much other people like these cards and agree on a fair trade. That's kind of like how Market Value works!

Market Value is like saying, "Hey, this card is worth a lot because a lot of people really want it!" So, when people trade or sell things, they use market value to decide what's a fair deal. It's like using a special guidebook to know how much something is worth in the big world of trading cards!

Marketing Strategy

Let's imagine you're a captain of a pirate ship. You want to find the best way to sail to a treasure island without getting caught by other pirates or bad weather. You plan which routes to take, when to set sail, and how to avoid dangers.

In business, a "marketing strategy" is a bit like your pirate plan. Companies use it to figure out the best way to reach their customers and sell their products. They decide which advertising methods to use, when to launch new products, and how to stand out from their competitors, just like you plan your pirate journey to find treasure!

Matrix Organization

Let's imagine a big treehouse with different levels. In each level, there are kids doing different activities. The top level is for drawing, the middle one for building with blocks, and the bottom for reading books.

Now, imagine if there were some kids who were really good at both drawing and building with blocks. They might spend time on both the top and middle levels. That's a bit like a "matrix organization" in a company.

In a matrix organization, people have two bosses or more, and they work on different projects at the same time. It's like being really good at both drawing and building, so you get to play on different levels of the treehouse!

Memorandum of Understanding (MOU)

Let's imagine you and your friend want to build a cool fort in the backyard. Before you start building, you both make a special promise. You write down what each of you is going to do, like who's in charge of finding blankets and who's in charge of finding sticks.

This special promise is like a "Memorandum of Understanding" or MOU in the corporate world. It's like a written plan that says, "You do this, and I'll do that," just like when you and your friend promise to do certain jobs to build your awesome fort!

Merger and Acquisition (M&A)

Let's imagine you have two teams in a big game. One team is really good at scoring goals, and the other team is super fast and great at passing the ball. They decide to team up and become even stronger by working together. That's kind of like what happens in a Merger and Acquisition!

A Merger and Acquisition is when two companies join forces, just like those two teams. One company might be really good at making awesome gadgets, and the other might be amazing at selling things all around the world. When they team up, they become one big super-team and work together to do even better in the business world!

Mindshare

Let's imagine you're at school with your friends. There's a new game that everyone is talking about. Even though you haven't played it yet, you're really curious and excited to try it out. Now, imagine a company makes a new toy or a game, and lots and lots of people all around the world get really curious and excited about it, just like you and your friends at school. That excitement and curiosity is a bit like what we call "mindshare" in the business world.

Mindshare is when a company's product or idea is so popular and talked about that it's on the minds of lots and lots of people. Just like how that new game was on your mind at school, some products or ideas can be on the minds of people all over the world!

Mission Statement

Let's pretend we're on a big adventure together! Imagine we're explorers setting out on a grand quest to find a legendary treasure. Now, before we set off, we gather around and talk about why this quest is important to us. We want to help people, discover new places, and make the world a better and happier place.

A mission statement is kind of like our adventurer's promise. It's a special message that a company writes down to explain why they exist and what they want to achieve. It's like their own quest to make the world better in some way, just like we want to make the world a better place by finding that legendary treasure!

MLS (Multiple Listing Service)

Let's play a game of treasure hunt with a twist! Imagine you're in a big park where there are lots of different trees. Each tree has a special secret hiding spot, and there's a map that shows where all these hiding spots are.

Now, the map is like an MLS (Multiple Listing Service). It helps you see all the cool hiding spots (like houses for sale) in the park. So, if you're looking for a special treasure (a new home), you can use the map to see all your options in one place, instead of wandering around the whole park. It's like a shortcut to finding what you're looking for!

Monetize

Let's imagine you have a special talent, like painting really awesome pictures. Now, imagine you have an art show where lots of people come to see your paintings. When someone really loves one of your paintings and wants to take it home, they give you some special coins in exchange for it. Those coins are like the way a company "monetizes" something.

So, when a company has something really cool, like a game or a video, they figure out a way to let people enjoy it and, in return, get something valuable back, like money. They're turning their awesome creations into something that helps them keep making more cool stuff!

Mortgage

Let's imagine you really want to build a cool treehouse in your backyard, but you don't have enough treehouse-building materials right now. So, your friend says, "Hey, I have some extra planks and nails. I'll give them to you, but you have to promise to give them back when you can."

That promise is like a "mortgage." It's an agreement you make with your friend to borrow the things you need for your treehouse. In the grown-up world, people might want to buy a house, but they don't have all the money right away. So, they make an agreement with a bank to borrow the money they need to buy the house, and they promise to pay it back over time. Just like you promised to give back the planks and nails to your friend!

Move the Needle

Imagine you and your friends are playing a game with a giant seesaw. The goal of the game is to make the seesaw tip all the way down on one side. But right now, it's perfectly balanced in the middle.

To "move the needle" in this game, you'd need to add more weight to one side. Let's say you and your friends start putting more and more rocks on one end. Slowly, the seesaw starts to tilt, and you can see it's not in the middle anymore. You've successfully "moved the needle"!

In business, when people say they want to "move the needle," they mean they want to make a big impact or achieve a significant change in a certain direction. It's like when a company wants to sell a lot more of their special toys. They'll come up with new and exciting ideas to make more kids want to play with them, and when they see their toy sales go way up, they can say, "We really moved the needle with our toy sales!"

Multinational Corporation (MNC)

Let's imagine a big pizza party! There's a special chef who makes delicious pizzas. This chef is so good that people from all over the world want to taste their pizzas.

Now, this chef doesn't just cook in one town. They have special pizza ovens set up in different cities all over the world. So, they're not just popular in one place, they're famous internationally!

A multinational corporation, or MNC, is kind of like that famous pizza chef. Instead of making pizzas, they sell products or offer services, and they have offices, stores, or factories in many different countries. So, they're not just a big deal in one city or country, but all over the world!

6

N, O, P, Q, R - Corporate Terms

Net Income

L et's embark on a little make-believe adventure! Imagine you have a super cool toy-making workshop. You create amazing toys and sell them to your friends. Each toy brings in some money, but you also have to buy the materials to make them, like wood, paint, and glue.

Let's say you made 20 awesome toys and sold them for a total of 100 dollars. But, remember, you spent 60 dollars on all the materials you used to make them.

Now, let's figure out how much money you've got in your pocket. You earned 100 dollars, but you spent 60 dollars on materials. So, how much is left for you?

Well, you have 40 dollars left after taking away the 60 dollars you spent. This 40 dollars is like your net income. It's the money you get to keep after covering all your toy-making costs.

In the big world of companies, net income is similar. It's the money they have left after they've paid for all the things they need to run their business. Just like in our toy workshop adventure, it's the profit they get to keep!

Net Profit Margin

Let's dive into a little make-believe again! Pretend you have a fantastic cookie-baking business. You make the most delicious cookies in the neighborhood and sell them to your friends. For every cookie you sell, you get some money, but you also have to spend a bit on the ingredients like flour, chocolate chips, and sugar.

Now, let's say you sold 50 cookies and earned 100 dollars. But, you spent 40 dollars on all the ingredients you used to make them.

Here's the cool part: the net profit margin is like figuring out how much money you made from each cookie after you've covered all your ingredient costs. It's kind of like seeing how much "extra" money you earned from each cookie.

So, if you earned 100 dollars from selling 50 cookies, that's 2 dollars for each cookie. After taking away the 40 dollars you spent on ingredients, you have 60 dollars left. That's like your "extra" money.

In the big world of companies, net profit margin is similar. It helps them see how much "extra" money they're making from each product they sell, after they've covered all their production costs. It's a way of figuring out how well their business is doing!

Net Promoter Score (NPS)

Let's imagine you have a new game that you really like playing. You show it to your friends and ask them if they like it too. Some of them say, "Wow, this game is awesome, I love it!" Others might say, "It's okay, not my favorite," and a few might say, "I don't really like it."

Your Net Promoter Score, or NPS, is like keeping track of how many friends really, really enjoy playing the game and would tell other friends to try it. It helps you see if lots of people love the game or if maybe you need to make it even more fun for everyone. So, if you have a high NPS, it's like knowing that your game is a big hit among your friends!

Non-Disclosure Agreement (NDA)

Let's pretend you and your friend have a super cool secret club. In order to join, your friend might ask you to promise that you won't tell anyone else about the secret handshake, the special password, or the clubhouse location. That promise is like a Non-Disclosure Agreement, or NDA.

It's a special kind of promise grown-ups use when they want to share exciting or important secrets with someone, but they need to make sure that person won't go and tell everyone else. So, just like in your secret club, the NDA helps keep things hush-hush!

Non-Governmental Organization (NGO)

Imagine you and your friends decide to start a super cool club to make your neighborhood even better. You're not a part of the official neighborhood council, but you still want to do awesome things like clean up the park, plant flowers, and have fun events.

That's kind of like what a Non-Governmental Organization, or NGO, does but on a bigger scale. NGOs are groups of people who come together to make positive changes in their community or even around the world. They work independently from the government, but they're still super helpful and do lots of good things, just like your neighborhood club!

Nonprofit Corporation

Let's imagine you and your friends are really good at baking delicious cookies. You decide to start a little cookie stand where you sell your cookies, but you don't want to keep all the money for yourselves. Instead, you want to use some of it to help people in need, like buying warm blankets for the homeless or books for a school that doesn't have many.

So, you and your friends form a special group called a "Nonprofit Corporation." It's like your cookie stand, but instead of keeping all the money for yourselves, you use it to do kind things for others. Just like how you share your cookie stand's earnings, a nonprofit corporation shares its earnings to help make the world a better place!

Nonprofit Organization

Imagine you and your friends love taking care of stray cats and dogs in your neighborhood. You feed them, build them cozy shelters, and make sure they're happy and safe. But you want to do even more! You decide to form a special group called a "Nonprofit Organization."

This is like creating a superhero team, but instead of fighting bad guys, you're all working together to help animals. You can raise money to buy food and medicine, build better shelters, and even find loving homes for the animals. Just like superheroes use their powers for good, a nonprofit organization uses its efforts to make the world a better place for animals and people!

Offer

Let's say you have a bunch of really cool trading cards, and your friend really, really wants one of them. They come up to you and say, "Hey, I'll trade you my super rare card for your awesome one!"

That's like making an "offer." It's like saying, "I'd like to make a deal!" In the business world, companies do this all the time. They might say, "Hey, we'll give you 10 of our cool toys if you give us 5 of your amazing games." It's a way of suggesting a trade or a deal to get something they want!

Offshoring

Let's pretend you have a magical treehouse where you make the most amazing drawings. You're super talented, and people from all over the neighborhood want your special drawings. But, there's a little problem – you're getting so many orders that it's hard to keep up.

Here's where offshoring comes in. Imagine if you had a team of magical helpers in another treehouse across the river. They're really good at drawing too, and you can teach them how to make your special drawings. So, you send some of your orders to them, and they help you out. That way, you can get more drawings done and make more people happy!

In the world of grown-up companies, offshoring is a bit like that. Sometimes, companies have tasks that they send to other places, usually in different countries, where there are skilled people who can help get the job done. It's like having a team of special helpers who work from a different location!

On the Same Page

Imagine you and your friends are putting together a big puzzle. You're all sitting around the table, trying to fit the pieces together to create an awesome picture.

Being "on the same page" means that everyone understands what the final picture should look like. It's like when you and your friends agree on which puzzle to do, and you all have the same idea about how it should look when it's finished. You're all working together towards the same goal, and that's what it means in the business world too – everyone understands and agrees on what needs to be done!

Operating Expenditure or Expenses (OpEx)

Let's imagine you have a lemonade stand. You've got your pitcher, cups, lemons, and sugar. These are all things you need to make and sell your lemonade. But remember, you'll have to buy more lemons and sugar when you run out, right?

Operating expenses, or OpEx, are like the things you need to keep your lemonade stand going. It's the money you spend on lemons, sugar, cups, and anything else you need to make and sell your lemonade. Just like you have to budget for these supplies to keep your stand running, a company has to plan for the money they'll spend on things like rent, salaries, and other day-to-day stuff to keep their business running smoothly.

Optimize

Let's imagine you're packing for a big trip to a magical amusement park. You have a backpack, and you want to fit as many fun things in there as possible - snacks, a water bottle, your favorite stuffed animal, and maybe a hat in case it gets sunny.

Now, you've got to be smart about how you pack it all. You'll arrange things so they fit just right, making sure nothing gets squished, and maybe even putting the heavier stuff on the bottom so it doesn't squash the snacks.

Optimizing in business is a bit like that. It means figuring out the best way to arrange or use things so everything works really well together. It's like making sure all the pieces in a puzzle fit just right, or packing your bag so you can bring as much fun as possible on your trip!

Organizational Chart

Let's imagine a big treehouse village. Each treehouse has a different job to do - one's a kitchen, one's a library, and another's a lookout post. Now, to make sure everything runs smoothly, the kids in the village draw a special map.

This map shows who's in charge of each treehouse and how they're connected. It's like a blueprint that helps everyone know where to go when they need something. That special map is a lot like an organizational chart in a company. It shows who's in charge of what and how they all work together to make things happen. Just like in the treehouse village, it helps everyone know who to talk to when they need something!

Organizational Culture

Let's pretend you're on a super cool sports team. Every player on the team has their own special way of playing, right? Some are really good at dribbling, others are awesome at passing, and a few are like super-speedy runners.

Now, imagine that your team has a special way of doing things – like before every game, you all have a special cheer that gets everyone pumped up. And after every game, win or lose, you all celebrate with a high-five tunnel. That's what makes your team unique, and it's something that everyone in the team follows.

Well, in companies, they also have a special way of doing things. It's like their own team cheer and high-five tunnel, but for work! This special way of doing things is called the "organizational culture." It's what makes each company special and sets it apart from others. Some companies might be really focused on teamwork, while others might be all about creativity and trying new things. Just like how every sports team has its own style, every company has its own unique way of working together.

Organizational Development (OD)

Alright, let's imagine you have a super cool clubhouse with all your friends. But as you grow, you realize you need to make it even better and more fun. So, you all gather and come up with awesome new ideas!

Some friends might suggest adding a secret passageway or making a cool mural. Others might think about how to make sure everyone's ideas get heard. This whole process of making your clubhouse better and helping it grow is a lot like what adults do in companies. When they work on making the company better and helping it grow, they call it Organizational Development (OD). It's like giving your clubhouse a super cool upgrade!

Organizational Structure

Let's pretend you're in charge of a big treehouse project with your friends. Everyone has a role to play, right? Some are in charge of gathering materials, others are great at building, and a few are like super organizers, making sure everything goes smoothly.

Now, let's say you decide that there should be a leader, sort of like a chief treehouse builder, who helps make the big decisions and keeps things running smoothly. Then, you have different groups for different tasks, like the Roof Team, the Decoration Team, and the Snack Team (because you'll need snacks, of course!).

This setup, with a leader and different teams, is a bit like how companies work. They have a structure, just like our treehouse project. There's usually a leader, called the CEO, who makes important decisions. Then there are different departments, like the Marketing Department, the Finance Department, and the Human Resources Department, each responsible for different parts of the company. This way, everyone knows their role and works together to build something amazing, just like in our treehouse project!

Outsource

Imagine you have a big group project with your friends. Each person has a special job to do to make the project amazing. But, let's say there's one part of the project that you're not an expert at, like drawing detailed maps. You remember that there's another group of friends who are really, really good at making awesome maps.

So, you decide to ask them for help. They join your project and take care of all the map-making. That way, everyone can focus on what they're best at, and the project turns out even better!

This is a bit like what companies do when they outsource. They ask other experts or groups to help with certain tasks, so they can make their overall project or product the absolute best it can be!

Pain Point

Let's imagine you're playing a board game with your friends. You're really close to winning, but there's one spot on the board that's a bit tricky. Every time you land on it, you have to go back a few spaces. It's like a thorn in your side, making it harder to reach the finish line.

In business, a "pain point" is like that tricky spot in the game. It's a problem or challenge that makes it harder for a company to reach its goals. Just like you want to get past that tricky spot in the game, companies want to find solutions to their pain points so they can reach their goals more easily!

Paradigm Shift

Imagine you're used to playing a certain type of video game. You're really good at it, and you know all the tricks and strategies. But one day, a brand new game comes out that's totally different. It's not like anything you've played before.

This new game requires you to use completely different skills and strategies. It's a whole new way of playing! That big change in how you approach games is a bit like a "paradigm shift" in the gaming world.

In business, a "paradigm shift" is when there's a big change in how things are done. It's like suddenly playing a whole new type of game in the business world. Companies might need to learn new ways of doing things, just like you had to learn new skills for the different video game.

Partnership

Let's imagine you and your best friend really love building things. You decide to team up and build amazing treehouses together. When you work together, you can use each other's ideas and skills to create something even better than you could on your own.

That's a bit like a partnership in business. It's when two or more people or companies join forces to work together. They bring their different strengths and ideas to create something awesome! Just like you and your friend build fantastic treehouses, in business, partners work together to achieve bigger and better things.

Patent

Let's go on a little adventure in your imagination! Imagine you're a super creative inventor, always coming up with amazing new toys and gadgets. Now, you want to make sure that no one else can copy your inventions because they're so special and unique.

So, just like when you draw a picture and put your name on it to say it's yours, inventors get something called a patent. It's like a special certificate from a grown-up group that says, "This amazing idea belongs to you, and no one else can use it without your permission!" It's like having a super special badge that shows everyone your cool invention is all yours.

Peer-to-Peer (P2P) Lending

Alright, let's imagine a big group of friends at a playground. Each friend has some cool toys, but one friend really wants to try a new game console. Now, instead of going to a store to buy it, they decide to do something different.

They decide to do a special kind of trade. They agree that one friend will let the other borrow their game console for a little while, and in return, the other friend will let them play with their collection of action figures. It's a fair exchange, and they both get to try something new!

That's a bit like what happens with Peer-to-Peer lending. It's when regular people like you and me lend money to each other, just like those friends at the playground trade toys. It helps people get what they need without always having to go to a big bank. Cool, right?

Performance Appraisal

Let's pretend you're a superhero, and you've just finished a big mission to save the city. Afterward, your team gathers around to talk about how everyone did.

Your leader says, "Okay, team, it's time for our Superhero Performance Appraisal!" They go over all the awesome things you did, like how fast you flew and how strong you were. They also talk about things that could be even better, like maybe learning a new move or working on teamwork.

It's like getting a report card, but for superheroing! The appraisal helps you see what you're really good at and what you can work on to become an even better superhero. In companies, they do something similar to see how well everyone is doing at their jobs. They talk about what's going great and what might need a little extra attention.

Personal Injury Law Firms

Let's imagine you're playing a game of tag with your friends in the park. Everyone is having a great time running around. Now, imagine someone accidentally trips and falls, and it hurts them. They have a little "ouchie." That's when someone who knows a lot about helping with ouchies comes in to help. They might clean up a scraped knee, put a bandage on, and make sure their friend is okay.

Well, personal injury law firms are a bit like those helpful friends. When someone gets hurt because of an accident or something that wasn't their fault, these law firms step in to help. They know a lot about the rules and laws that can make things better for the person who got hurt. It's like having a team of really knowledgeable friends who want to make sure everyone gets the help they need after an accident.

Pre-Approval

Let's imagine you're planning a big sleepover party with your friends. You've asked your parents if it's okay, but they want to know who's coming and what you'll be doing to make sure everything is safe and fun.

So, they give you a "pre-approval." It's like a special permission slip that says, "If you follow these rules and plans, then the party can happen." It's like getting the green light before the actual event. That way, everyone knows what to expect and can have a great time!

Price-Earnings Ratio (P/E Ratio)

Let's imagine you have a collection of trading cards. Each card is like a tiny piece of a company. Now, imagine you want to know if one card is more valuable than another.

The "Price-Earnings Ratio" is like a special number that helps you figure out which card might be more valuable. It's like looking at how many cool features a card has compared to how much it costs to get that card. If a card has lots of cool features but doesn't cost too much, it might have a high Price-Earnings Ratio, which means it could be a really good deal!

Principal

Let's imagine you have a treehouse club with your friends. In this club, everyone has different jobs. The leader of the club, who makes the big decisions and keeps everyone in line, is like the "Principal" of a school.

Just like your treehouse club wouldn't run smoothly without a leader, a school needs a principal to make sure everything is going well and everyone is learning and playing nicely together. They're like the captain of the ship, steering it in the right direction!

Private Equity

Imagine you have a super cool clubhouse in your backyard. It's a special place where you and your friends come up with awesome ideas for games and projects. Now, let's say you want to build something really amazing, like a super-duper treehouse with a zip line, but you need some extra money for all the cool stuff.

That's where the "Private Equity" comes in. It's like having a super generous aunt or uncle who believes in your treehouse dreams. They give you some extra money so you can build the most epic treehouse ever! In the business world, "Private Equity" is like having really supportive grown-ups who invest in cool ideas and help them grow into something even more amazing.

Probate

Alright, let's imagine your family has a really special treasure chest. It's filled with all sorts of treasures, like old maps, shiny jewels, and maybe even some secret messages. Now, let's say the person who knows all about these treasures isn't around anymore. That's where "Probate" comes in.

Probate is like having a wise and fair judge who looks at all the treasures and makes sure they go to the right people. They make sure everyone gets their fair share and that everything is done just the way it's supposed to be. So, probate is like having a really trustworthy treasure guardian who makes sure everything is in order.

Procurement

Let's imagine you're the captain of a pirate ship. Your job is to gather all the supplies you need for your crew's big adventure on the high seas. You have to find the best maps, the sturdiest swords, and the yummiest food. That's a bit like what "procurement" means in the business world.

In a company, there are people whose job is to find and get all the things the company needs, just like you finding maps, swords, and food for your pirate crew. They make sure everything is of good quality and the best value, so the company can do its job just like your crew needs the best gear for their voyage.

Product Development

Let's say you're a brilliant young inventor, always coming up with amazing ideas for toys and games. You've got a wild imagination and love creating new things.

Now, you've got this fantastic idea for a brand new type of game. It's a mix of a board game and a scavenger hunt, and you're sure it's going to be a huge hit. But here's the thing: you've got the idea, but turning it into a real, playable game takes a lot of work.

You need to design the game board, create the rules, draw the cards, and make sure everything works smoothly. So, you gather a team of your friends who are really good at drawing, writing, and problem-solving. Each one helps bring a different part of the game to life.

That whole process of turning your awesome idea into a real, playable game is a bit like what happens in a company when they're working on a new product. They start with a great idea, just like you did. Then, they gather a team of experts who each have their own special skills, like designing, engineering, and testing, to bring that idea to life. It's like a big, creative adventure!

Product Development Lifecycle (PDLC)

Let's imagine you're an artist. You start with a blank canvas, and you have this idea in your head about what you want to paint. First, you sketch out the basic shapes, just like when a company gets an idea for a new product. Then, you start adding colors and details, making it better and better. This is like the different stages in a product's development.

After a while, your painting is finished, and it's ready to be shown to the world.

Similarly, in a company, once a product has gone through all the stages of development and is just right, it's ready to be released and used by people. The whole process from the first idea to the finished product is called the Product Development Lifecycle, or PDLC for short.

Product Differentiation

Let's pretend you and your friends all have a big box of crayons. You decide to draw pictures, but you want your drawing to stand out. So, you choose to use glitter and stickers on top of your crayon colors. This makes your picture look different and special compared to your friends' drawings.

In a similar way, when companies make products, they want them to stand out from similar products made by other companies. They do this by adding special features, designs, or qualities that make their product different and unique. This is called "product differentiation." It's like giving your drawing that extra sparkle to make it special!

Professional (vs. Expert)

Imagine we're talking about video games.

A "Professional" gamer is like someone who's really, really good at playing a specific game. They practice a lot and compete in big tournaments. They're like the top players in a sports league, earning prizes and recognition for their amazing skills.

On the other hand, an "Expert" gamer is someone who knows a whole bunch about all sorts of games. They might not be at the pro level in one particular game, but they understand games really well. They're like the wise wizards of the gaming world, helping others become better players.

So, a "Professional" is like the superstar of one game, while an "Expert" is like the wise guru who knows a lot about many games! They both bring something special to the gaming world.

In a nutshell, a Professional gets paid for their work, while an Expert is skilled at work.

Professional Corporation (PC)

Imagine you and your friends love building treehouses. You decide to form a special club just for treehouse builders. This club is called the "Treehouse Pros Club" or "TPC" for short.

Now, in a similar way, when grown-ups like lawyers, doctors, or accountants want to work together, they might form a special group called a "Professional Corporation" or "PC." It's like your Treehouse Pros Club, but for grown-ups who are really good at their jobs! They work together to help people and make sure everything is done just right.

Profit Margin

Alright, let's pretend you have a lemonade stand. You sell cups of lemonade for 50 cents each, and it costs you 30 cents to make each cup. That means you make 20 cents in profit for every cup you sell.

Your profit margin is like looking at how much money you make compared to how much it costs to make the lemonade. It's like saying, "For every dollar I spend making lemonade, how much do I get back when I sell it?"

So, if you're making a lot more than you're spending, you have a good profit margin! It's like saying your lemonade stand is doing really well and making a nice amount of money.

Project Management

Let's imagine you're the captain of a spaceship on a mission to explore a new planet. Your job is to make sure everything goes smoothly from launch to landing.

Being a project manager is a bit like being the captain. You have to plan out every step, make sure everyone knows what they're supposed to do, and keep an eye on the schedule to make sure you arrive on the new planet right on time.

If something unexpected happens, like an asteroid coming too close, you need to figure out a solution quickly so it doesn't mess up the whole mission. And you always keep your crew updated about what's going on.

So, project management is like being the space captain, making sure every-thing goes according to plan on a big adventure!

Proxy Statement

Let's say you and your friends decide to have a super important meeting to plan a big adventure. But, here's the twist - one of your friends can't make it to the meeting. Oh no!

So, what do you do? You ask your friend to write down all their ideas, thoughts, and suggestions about the adventure. Then, during the meeting, another friend reads out what was written, making sure everyone knows what the absent friend wants.

A proxy statement in the corporate world is a bit like this. Imagine a big company is having a super important meeting, just like you and your friends. Sometimes, a shareholder (someone who owns part of the company) can't make it to the meeting. So, they write down all their thoughts, ideas, and what they want to say about the company. This is called a proxy statement.

Then, when the meeting happens, someone reads out the proxy statement to make sure everyone knows what the absent shareholder thinks. It's like making sure everyone's voice is heard, even if they can't be there in person!

Public Corporation

Imagine a big amusement park that's open for everyone to visit. It's like a huge playground with lots of rides and games. This amusement park is owned by many people, and anyone can come in and have fun.

A public corporation is kind of like that amusement park. It's a big company that's owned by lots and lots of people, and anyone can buy a little piece of it. Just like how you can get a ticket to the amusement park and enjoy all the rides, people can buy shares of a public corporation and be a part-owner of the company.

So, a public corporation is like a super-sized amusement park that's open for everyone to join in and be a part of the fun!

Push the Envelope

Let's imagine you have a big stack of building blocks. Usually, you build things by following the instructions, right? But sometimes, you want to see how tall and amazing you can make your tower. So, you start stacking the blocks higher and higher, even though it's a bit risky.

Pushing the envelope in business is a bit like that. It means trying new and bold things, even if they might be a little risky. It's like going beyond the usual way of doing things to see if you can make something really impressive and special. Just like with your tower of blocks!

Quality Control

Let's pretend you're a baker. When you make cookies, you want to make sure they're the best they can be, right? So, after you mix the dough and shape the cookies, you carefully check them before they go into the oven. You want them to be just right – not too big, not too small, and definitely not burnt!

Quality control in business is a bit like that. It means checking and testing products or services to make sure they're really good before they go out to customers. Just like you inspect your cookies to make sure they're perfect, businesses have teams that check their products to make sure they're top-notch. They want everything to be just right, just like your cookies!

Quick Wins

Alright, imagine you have a big pile of homework to do, and it looks a little overwhelming. But you notice that one of the exercises is really easy and you can finish it super quickly. So, you decide to do that one first. Boom! You've got one task done, and it feels great!

In business, 'quick wins' are a bit like that easy homework exercise. They're small tasks or projects that a company can do pretty fast, and they usually bring in positive results. It's like getting a little victory that gives everyone a boost of energy and confidence to tackle the bigger tasks ahead. Just like finishing that easy homework makes the rest seem less daunting!

Raise the Bar

Let's pretend you're playing a game where you jump over a bar that keeps getting higher. At first, it's set at a height that's easy for you to clear. But then, as you keep jumping successfully, the game gets more challenging and they raise the bar higher and higher!

In business, when people say "raise the bar," they mean setting higher standards or aiming for even better results. It's like always trying to do your best and then challenging yourself to do even better next time. Just like in the game, you're constantly pushing yourself to reach new heights!

Real Estate

Imagine a big puzzle made of different pieces. Each piece is like a part of a town or a city, with houses, schools, parks, and stores. Now, think of real estate like owning one or more of those puzzle pieces.

When someone talks about real estate, they're talking about land and buildings. It's like having a piece of the puzzle that you can use in different ways. Some people might build houses or apartments on their piece, while others might put up stores or offices. It's like having your very own spot in the big puzzle of a town!

Real Estate Agent

Let's pretend you're hosting a big treasure hunt in your neighborhood. You've hidden lots of cool prizes, but you need someone to help you give out clues and make sure everything runs smoothly.

A real estate agent is a bit like that helper. They're experts who help people find or sell houses. They know all the nooks and crannies of the neighborhood and can give you clues about which houses might be the best fit for you. They're like the treasure hunt guide for grown-ups looking for their perfect home!

Real Estate Law Firms

Imagine you and your friends are playing a big game in your neighborhood. You want to make sure everyone follows the rules and there are no arguments. So, you ask a wise grown-up, like a real estate law firm, to be the referee.

They know all the rules about buying and selling houses and can help make sure everything is fair and square, just like a good referee in a game!

Registered (vs. Licensed)

Let's imagine you have a super cool clubhouse with a special rule: only members are allowed inside. To become a member, your friends need to officially sign up, like writing their name on a special list. Once they're on that list, they're considered "registered" members and can come in anytime.

Now, think of a different scenario. Imagine you have a bunch of amazing toys, and you let your friends borrow them sometimes, but they have to promise to bring them back. This promise is like a special agreement, and we call it a "license." It's like saying, "Sure, you can borrow my toy, but you have to follow these rules."

So, when something is "registered," it means it's officially on a list, like members in your clubhouse. When something is "licensed," it means there's a special agreement in place, like lending toys to your friends. Both are ways of making things official, just in different ways!

Registered Trademark (vs. Trademark)

Let's imagine you have a super special drawing you made, and you want everyone to know it's yours. So, you put your secret artist symbol on it. Now, no one else can use that symbol because it's yours! That special symbol is like a "Trademark."

But let's say you want to make extra sure that nobody else can use your symbol. So, you go to the official Art Museum and show them your symbol. They say, "Wow, this is amazing! It's now in our special book of super-duper symbols, and it's called a 'Registered Trademark'!" This means it's extra, extra protected and officially recognized. So, no one can use it without asking you first!

Registration

Let's imagine you're having a big birthday party. You want to make sure all your friends know about it, right? So, you make special invitations with all the details like date, time, and place. Now, when your friends get these invitations, they know they're officially invited to the party!

In the corporate world, "registration" is a bit like sending out those special invitations. It's when a company officially tells the world about something important they're doing, like starting a new project or claiming ownership of something they've created. It's like saying, "Hey everyone, look, this is ours!" Just like your birthday party, it makes things official!

Research and Development (R&D)

Imagine you're a scientist in a big kitchen. Your job is to create new recipes for delicious cookies. You spend lots of time experimenting with different ingredients, like chocolate chips, peanut butter, and sprinkles, to make the tastiest cookies ever. That's a bit like what research and development (R&D) is for companies. They have special teams of people who work like scientists, trying out new ideas and inventions to come up with exciting products that people will love, just like you love those yummy cookies!

Resource Allocation

Let's picture this: You're a captain of a spaceship, and you have a limited amount of fuel to reach your destination. You also have to decide how much fuel to use for each part of the journey – taking off, cruising, and landing. If you use too much at the beginning, you might not have enough to finish the trip!

In a company, resource allocation is a bit like that. Instead of fuel, it's money, time, and people. The leaders have to decide how much of these resources to use for different projects, making sure there's enough to finish everything successfully. Just like you have to manage your spaceship's fuel, they have to manage the company's resources!

Rest and Relaxation (R&R)

Let's go on an adventure in our imaginary Forest of Work and Play. Imagine you're like a busy little squirrel, always running around, gathering nuts, and building nests. It's hard work, and you get pretty tired!

But even squirrels need a break, right? So, sometimes, you find a cozy spot in the forest where you can take a little rest. You stretch out, close your eyes, and just enjoy the peacefulness for a while. That's your Rest and Relaxation time!

In companies, people work really hard, just like our little squirrel. They're always doing important tasks. But just like that squirrel needs a break, so do the people at work. That's when they get some Rest and Relaxation time to recharge their energy and come back even stronger for their next adventure in the Forest of Work and Play!

Restricted Stock Units (RSUs)

Imagine you're a young wizard in a magical world. Instead of getting your magical powers all at once, you receive special crystals called RSUs from a wise old wizard. These crystals have incredible powers, but you can't use them right away.

Each year, the old wizard lets you harness a portion of the crystal's power. So, as time passes, you become more and more powerful. But, here's the thing - if you ever leave the magical school, you can only take the powers you've earned so far. The rest stay with the school.

In the world of companies, RSUs are like magical crystals that a company gives its employees. They promise special rewards, but the employees can only use them over time. If they leave the company early, they only get to keep what they've "earned" so far. It's a bit like being a wizard in a magical school!

Results-Driven

Okay, imagine you're on a soccer team, and your team really wants to win the championship. Being results-driven is like having a scoreboard in your mind that shows how many goals your team has scored.

So, instead of just playing for fun, you and your teammates are super focused on winning. You practice hard, come up with strategies, and always try your best during the games to get those goals on the scoreboard. That's being results-driven in soccer!

In the business world, being results-driven means that people are really focused on achieving their goals and getting things done, just like scoring goals in soccer. They work hard and stay determined to see those results on their "scoreboard" at work.

Return on Assets (ROA)

Let's think of your toys at home as a business. Imagine you have a bunch of different toys, like action figures, board games, and building blocks. These toys are like the assets of your "toy business."

Now, let's say you want to know how well your toy business is doing. To figure this out, you look at how much fun you're having with your toys compared to how many toys you have. If you're having a lot of fun with all your toys, you're getting a good "return" on your toys, right? That's like having a high Return on Assets in a business.

But if you have a lot of toys and you're not really playing with them much, then you're not getting as much "return" on your toys. It's kind of like having a big collection of action figures but not really enjoying them. In business, that would mean the Return on Assets is lower.

So, Return on Assets is like figuring out how well you're using all your toys to have a good time! In a real business, they use it to see how well they're using their stuff, like buildings, machines, and money, to make a profit.

Return on Equity (ROE)

Alright, let's think of a lemonade stand as a little business. You and your friend decide to start a lemonade stand. You both put in some money to buy lemons, sugar, and cups. That's like the "equity" in your business.

Now, after a busy day of selling lemonade, you count up all the money you made. Let's say you made a good amount of profit. That's like the extra money you have after you've paid for all the supplies. In business terms, that's your "return."

Return on Equity, or ROE, is like looking at how much extra money you made compared to how much you and your friend put in at the start. If you made a lot of extra money compared to what you started with, your lemonade stand has a high Return on Equity. It means your business is doing really well!

But if you didn't make much extra money, then the Return on Equity isn't as high. It's like saying your lemonade stand didn't make a big profit compared to what you and your friend invested. So, ROE helps people see how good a business is at using the money it started with to make even more money!

Return on Investment (ROI)

Imagine you love trading your toys. You know which toys are super popular and can be traded for more cool toys later. So, you decide to trade your rare action figure for three other awesome toys.

Later on, you notice that those three toys are really popular too! You can trade them for even more toys! This time, you get five toys in return. That's like making a profit!

Return on Investment, or ROI, is a bit like keeping track of how many extra toys you got from your original action figure trade. It helps you see if your trading decisions are super smart or if you might want to try a different approach next time.

If you keep making trades that give you lots of extra toys, your ROI is high.

That means you're really good at picking toys to trade! But if you end up with only a few extra toys, your ROI isn't as high. It's like saying you might want to rethink your trading strategy. So, ROI helps people figure out how well their investments (like trading toys) are working out.

Return on Investment Capital (ROIC)

Let's imagine you have a big jar of special marbles, and you want to use them to build something amazing, like a marble tower. But here's the tricky part: you can only use a certain number of marbles at a time, and you want to make sure you're using them really wisely.

So, you start building your tower, carefully placing marbles one by one. When you're finished, you step back and see how tall and sturdy it is compared to the number of marbles you used.

Return on Investment Capital, or ROIC, is a bit like measuring how tall and strong your marble tower is compared to the marbles you used. It helps you see if you're using your marbles (which represent the resources you have) in the most efficient and effective way.

If your tower is super tall and impressive for the number of marbles you used, your ROIC is high. That means you're really good at building with your resources! But if your tower isn't as impressive for the marbles you used, your ROIC isn't as high. It's like saying you might want to try a different approach next time. So, ROIC helps people figure out how well they're using their resources to build something great.

Return on Sales (ROS)

Let's imagine you have a lemonade stand. You sell cups of lemonade to your friends and neighbors. Now, you want to know if you're making a good amount of money for all the cups you sell.

Return on Sales, or ROS, is like looking at your lemonade stand and seeing if you're making a good profit. It helps you figure out if you're getting enough money back from all the cups of lemonade you're selling.

If you're making a lot of money for every cup of lemonade you sell, your ROS is high. It means you're doing a great job at turning your lemons into cash! But if you're not making much money for each cup, your ROS isn't as high. That's like saying you might want to think about your prices or find ways to sell more.

So, ROS helps you see if your lemonade stand is making a good profit, just like in business, it helps companies see if they're making a good profit from all the things they sell.

Revenue

Let's go on a little adventure! Pretend you have a super cool lemonade stand. You make the best lemonade in town. One sunny day, lots of people come to buy your lemonade, and they each give you a little bit of money.

Now, let's say you counted all the money you made in a day. That total amount of money you earned from selling your lemonade is like your revenue. It's the total amount of money that came in from all your sales.

In the business world, companies have their own "lemonade stands" where they sell products or provide services. The money they earn from these sales is their revenue. Just like you, they want to know how much they're making to see if their business is doing well!

Revenue Growth

Imagine you have a garden where you grow all sorts of colorful flowers. Every year, more and more flowers bloom, and your garden gets bigger and more beautiful.

Now, think of a company's Revenue Growth like the growth of your flower garden. Instead of flowers, it's the money a company makes from selling things. When a company has good Revenue Growth, it means they're selling more and more stuff each year, just like your garden is growing more and more flowers.

But sometimes, if the weather isn't great, or if you forget to water your garden, it might not grow as much. Similarly, if a company isn't doing well or if people aren't interested in their products, their Revenue Growth might not be as impressive.

So, Revenue Growth helps us see how well a company is doing in selling its products or services, just like your garden shows how well you're growing beautiful flowers.

Revenue Recognition

Let's imagine you have a lemonade stand. You sell lemonades to your neighbors, and you're really good at it! But you don't just count the money as soon as someone gives it to you. Instead, you keep track of how many lemonades you sold each day.

At the end of the day, you write down in your special notebook how much money you made and how many lemonades you sold. This way, you know exactly how well your lemonade stand is doing.

In the world of companies, Revenue Recognition is a bit like that special notebook. When a company sells something, they don't just say "Yay, we made money!" right away. They keep track of what they've sold and when they can officially count it as money they've earned. This helps them see how well they're doing and make smart decisions for the future.

Revenue Streams

Let's embark on a little pretend adventure. Imagine you're a super imaginative artist, and you have a bunch of different ways you can sell your amazing artwork. You could have a booth at the local art fair, sell paintings online, or even offer art classes to other kids in your neighborhood.

Each of these ways you sell your art is like a little stream of money flowing into your art business. Just like a river has different streams that flow into it, your art business has different "revenue streams" that bring in money.

Companies in the business world also have different ways they make money. They might sell products, offer services, or even license their ideas to other companies. Each of these ways is like a different stream of revenue flowing into their business.

So, when we talk about "revenue streams" in the business world, we're basically talking about all the different ways a company makes money, just like all the different ways you can sell your fantastic artwork!

Risk Management

Alright, let's picture you're planning a big adventure in the forest. You're super excited, but you also know that there might be some unexpected things that could happen, like getting lost or encountering wild animals.

So, what do you do? You pack a special backpack with things like a map, a compass, a whistle, and even a first-aid kit. These are your tools to help you stay safe and handle any surprises that might come your way.

In the corporate world, Risk Management is a bit like your special backpack. When companies have big plans, they know that there could be unexpected challenges or problems along the way. So, just like you pack your backpack with tools for your adventure, companies have strategies and plans in place to handle any unexpected situations that might come up. This way, they can stay safe and keep moving forward, just like you in the forest!

Runway

Let's imagine you're playing with a toy car on a really long track. The track stretches out ahead of you, and you can see it going on for a long, long way.

In the corporate world, a "runway" is like that long track for a company. It's the amount of time a company has before it needs to make more money or reach a goal. Imagine the company is like the toy car, and the runway is the track it's traveling on. If the track is really long, the company has plenty of time to reach its goal. But if the track is short, the company needs to go faster to reach the finish line in time. So, when people talk about a company's "runway," they're talking about how much time it has to get where it wants to go.

7

S, T, U, V, W, X, Y, Z - Corporate Terms

S Corporation (S Corp)

L et's pretend you and your friends have a clubhouse where you all play and share toys. Now, imagine if your clubhouse had special rules. These rules make sure everyone gets a fair turn and helps decide what games you play.

An S Corporation (S Corp) is a bit like a special clubhouse for grown-up businesses. It has certain rules that help the owners, or shareholders, share the toys (or profits) in a fair way and decide what "games" (or activities) the company will do.

So, just like your special clubhouse rules make sure everyone has a good time, S Corporations have rules that help the owners run their business in a fair and organized way.

Seamless

Let's imagine you're playing with a set of building blocks, just like those colorful ones you have at home. Now, when you're building something really cool with your blocks, it's like putting them together without any gaps or spaces between them. Everything fits perfectly, and it looks super smooth.

When people in the business world talk about something being "seamless," they mean that different parts of a project or a system fit together perfectly, just like your building blocks. It's like when all the pieces work together smoothly without any bumps or hiccups, making everything easy and efficient. So, "seamless" in business is like your awesome block creation— everything just clicks into place perfectly.

Security Token Offering (STO)

Imagine you have a special kind of treasure chest. But instead of holding gold coins, it holds something even more special: tokens! These tokens represent a share of ownership in something really cool, like a magical adventure park.

Now, let's say you want to invite some of your friends to be co-owners of this adventure park. You can give them some of these special tokens from your treasure chest. This is a bit like a "Security Token Offering" in the business world. It's when a company gives out special tokens to people who want to be part-owners of something amazing, like your magical adventure park.

So, just like you share tokens to let your friends join in the fun, companies use Security Token Offerings to let people become part-owners of their exciting projects!

Seller's Agent

Let's pretend you have a really cool trading card. It's super rare and everyone wants it. Now, there's a friend of yours who knows a lot about trading cards and how much they're worth. You ask this friend to help you sell your super special card.

This friend is like a "Seller's Agent" in the world of trading cards. They're an expert at getting the best deal for your card because they know all the ins and outs of the trading card market. They'll help you find the right buyer and make sure you get a fair price.

So, a Seller's Agent is like having a really knowledgeable friend who helps you get the most out of selling something valuable, just like your amazing trading card!

Seller's Market

Imagine you have a collection of super cool stickers that everyone really wants. You're the only one in the neighborhood who has them, so everyone is coming to you, asking if they can trade for your stickers.

Since you're the only sticker source around, you get to pick and choose which stickers you want in return. You have the upper hand in the trades because everyone really wants what you have.

That's kind of like a "Seller's Market" in the world of stickers. When it's a seller's market, the person who has the special stuff has a lot of power because everyone is trying to get it. They can ask for what they want in return!

So, a seller's market is like being the one with the most awesome stickers in the whole neighborhood!

Service Level Agreement (SLA)

Let's imagine you have a secret clubhouse with some rules. Everyone who wants to join the clubhouse has to follow these rules, like being nice to each other and cleaning up after themselves.

A Service Level Agreement, or SLA, is kind of like the rules for your clubhouse. It's an agreement between two parties that lays out what each of them is supposed to do. For example, if you have a computer game, the SLA might say that if the game stops working, the company promises to fix it within a certain amount of time.

Just like in your clubhouse, where everyone has to follow the rules, in a Service Level Agreement, everyone has to do what they promised. It's like a promise contract to make sure things run smoothly and everyone is happy!

Share Buyback

Alright, let's pretend you have a collection of trading cards. Sometimes, you might decide that you want to get some cards back that you traded away before. So, you offer your friends a deal: you'll give them some of your extra cards in exchange for the ones you want back.

In the business world, when a company does a "Share Buyback," it's a bit like you trading cards with your friends. The company decides to buy back some of its own shares from people who own them. This way, they have fewer shares out there, kind of like you having fewer cards in your collection.

Just like you might want certain cards back for your collection, a company might have its own reasons for wanting to buy back its shares. Maybe they think it's a good deal, or they want to make their remaining shares more valuable. It's all part of the big game of business!

Shareholder Activism

Pretend you and your friends are all part of a big club. In this club, you make decisions about what games to play and what activities to do together. Most of the time, everyone agrees and has a great time.

But one day, you notice that some of your friends want to play different games or do different things. They speak up and say, "Hey, let's try this new game!" or "How about we have a special art day?" They're being active and making their voices heard.

In a big company, there are people who own a part of the company. They're called shareholders. They're like members of a club, but instead of deciding games, they help make big decisions about the company, like who should be in charge and what direction the company should go in.

Shareholder activism is when these owners, the shareholders, start speaking up and suggesting changes in the way the company is run. It's like your friends in the club saying, "Hey, let's try something different!" They're being active in how the company works, just like your friends suggesting new games to play.

Shareholder Value

Let's say you have a magical tree in your backyard. This tree grows delicious apples. Every time you pick an apple and share it with your friends, everyone is happy and has a great time. The tree's value isn't just in the apples, but in the joy it brings to you and your friends.

In a big company, like the one that makes your favorite toys, they have something special too. It's called shareholder value. It's like the magic of the apple tree, but instead of apples, it's about how happy and successful the company makes its owners, who are like the gardeners of this big company.

When a company does well and makes smart choices, it's like the tree growing lots of sweet apples. This makes the owners, or shareholders, really happy because the company becomes even more valuable. Just like you and your friends enjoy the apples, the shareholders enjoy the success of the company. That's what we mean by shareholder value. It's the special magic that makes everyone smile!

Six Sigma

Let's pretend you're a super-duper master builder, like a wizard with blocks. You've noticed that sometimes, when you build big towers, they end up a little wobbly or not quite perfect. That's okay, but you want to be even better, right?

So, you start using a special technique called "Six Sigma." It's like having a magical ruler that helps you measure everything super precisely. With Six Sigma, you're able to build towers that are incredibly straight and just about as perfect as can be.

In the business world, when people talk about Six Sigma, they mean using special techniques to make sure everything runs super smoothly and perfectly. Just like you with your building blocks, companies use Six Sigma to make sure their processes are as close to perfect as possible!

Smart Contracts

Imagine you have a magical diary. This diary is super special because it follows instructions all by itself. You write down what you want, and the diary makes it happen, like magic!

Smart contracts in business are a bit like that magical diary. They're like special computer programs that follow instructions automatically. When certain conditions are met, they make things happen without anyone needing to do it manually. It's like having a little helper that knows exactly what to do when certain things occur!

Sole Proprietorship

Let's imagine you have a lemonade stand. You make the lemonade, set up the stand, and collect the money all by yourself. It's your own little business, and you're in charge of everything.

A sole proprietorship is a bit like your lemonade stand. It's a type of business where one person is in charge of everything. They come up with the ideas, do the work, and make all the decisions. It's like being the boss of your own lemonade empire!

Solvency Ratio

Let's imagine you have a really big jar of candies. You also have a bunch of friends who know you're good at sharing. You want to make sure you have enough candies to give to everyone and still have some left for yourself.

The solvency ratio is a bit like that. It's a way to see if a company has enough "candies" (or money) to pay off all its debts and still have some left over. It's like checking if you have enough candies to share with your friends and keep some for yourself too!

Sovereign Wealth Fund

Let's imagine you have a super-duper special treasure chest. But instead of just keeping it in your room, you decide to put it in a really safe and special place, like a super-duper high-tech vault.

Now, imagine that a whole bunch of kids in your neighborhood want to keep their special treasures safe too. So, you decide to let them put their treasure chests in your super-duper vault. You promise to take really good care of them.

A Sovereign Wealth Fund is kind of like that super-duper vault, but for a whole country! It's like a giant treasure chest where a country puts some of its special money to keep it safe and maybe even make it grow bigger over time. It's like a super-safe place for a whole country's special treasures!

Span of Control

Let's imagine you're the captain of a pirate ship. You have a crew of other pirates who help you sail the ship, find treasure, and have grand adventures.

Now, imagine if you had a whole bunch of pirate crews, each with their own captains. You're the big boss pirate overseeing all of them. The number of crews you can effectively manage is like your "span of control." If you have too many crews to look after, things might get a bit chaotic, and you might not be able to give each crew the attention and guidance they need.

So, your "span of control" is like how many pirate crews you can lead and still make sure everything runs smoothly!

Spin-Off

Pretend you have a box of colorful crayons. You love all the colors, but there are some that you like to use together more often. One day, you decide to take out a few of those special colors and put them in a new box, so they have their own space to shine.

A spin-off in the business world is a bit like that. Imagine a big company that makes toys and video games. They might have a special part of their business that's like those special colors of crayons. It's so unique and important that they decide to let it have its own box, or in this case, its own separate company.

Just like you made a new box for your favorite crayons, the big company makes a new company for that special part of their business. This way, it can grow and shine on its own, just like those special colors in your crayon box. That's what we mean by a spin-off - giving something special its own space to grow and be amazing!

Stakeholder

Pretend you're the captain of a pirate ship. You've got your crew, your treasure map, and your trusty parrot. Now, think about all the people who care about what you're doing as a pirate.

Your crewmates, of course, are some of the most important. They help you steer the ship, find treasure, and keep an eye out for other ships. They're like your team members on a big project.

But there are other folks who are interested too. The villagers in the towns you visit might hope you won't cause trouble, while other pirates might be eyeing your treasure with envy. Even the animals and creatures of the sea might have a stake in what you're up to.

All these different groups of people and creatures who care about what you're doing are like stakeholders in a company. They all have an interest in what happens, and they might be affected by the decisions you make. So, in the world of business, a stakeholder is anyone who has a 'stake' or an interest in how a company does. Just like on your pirate ship, it's important to consider what all these different groups think and want. That's how you keep everyone happy and the ship sailing smoothly!

Stakeholder Engagement

Let's pretend you're the captain of a big treehouse. You built it with the help of your friends and you all love playing in it. Now, imagine that there's a big, friendly squirrel who lives nearby, and a kind owl that visits sometimes.

You really care about what the squirrel and owl think about your treehouse, so you talk to them and ask if they like it or if they have any suggestions. You're making sure they're happy and involved in what happens with the treehouse.

This is a bit like "stakeholder engagement" in companies. The people who care about what the company does, like customers, employees, and even people in the community nearby, are like the squirrel and owl. Companies talk to them and listen to their ideas to make sure everyone is happy and things are going well, just like you do with your treehouse friends!

Statement of Cash Flows

Let's imagine you're the manager of a lemonade stand. You have a special book where you write down all the money that comes in (when people buy lemonade) and all the money that goes out (like when you buy lemons and cups). This special book helps you see if you're making a profit or if you need to make some changes.

A "Statement of Cash Flows" is like that special book for bigger companies. They use it to keep track of all the money they get from selling things and all the money they spend on different parts of the business. It helps them see if they're doing well and if they need to make any changes, just like your special book helps you with your lemonade stand!

Statutory Close Corporation

Alright, let's imagine a Statutory Close Corporation like a very special club. This club is not like the big clubs where lots of people can join. No, this club is small and only a few very close friends or family members can be part of it.

In this special club, everyone has an important role and they all work together to make decisions. It's like when you and your close friends decide what games to play or what movies to watch together. And just like in the club, decisions in this type of corporation are made by a small group of people who are really close and trust each other. They work together to make the best choices for their business.

Stock Options

Imagine stock options like a special kind of coupon. You know how sometimes you get a coupon for a free ice cream cone or a toy at a store? Well, stock options are like coupons for owning a tiny piece of a big company.

So, let's say you really like a cool toy store, and they give you a special coupon. This coupon says that one day, when you're a bit older, you can get a small piece of the toy store. That's what stock options do for grown-ups with big companies. It's like a special way for them to say, "Hey, one day you can own a piece of our company too!" Cool, right?

Strategic Alliance

Let's imagine you and your best friend both love building awesome things. You're really good at building cool towers, and your friend is amazing at making bridges. Now, instead of just building separately, you decide to team up and make something super-duper amazing!

That's kind of like a strategic alliance in the business world. It's when two companies, kind of like you and your friend, decide to work together because they're really good at different things. By teaming up, they can make something even more fantastic than they could on their own! So, it's like saying, "Hey, let's join forces and make something incredible!" Cool, right?

Strategic Planning

Let's pretend you're going on a big adventure, like a quest to find hidden treasures. You wouldn't just start running in any direction, right? You'd sit down with a map, maybe draw out a plan, and figure out the best path to take. You'd think about what you might need, like a flashlight, snacks, and a trusty sidekick.

Strategic planning in business is a bit like that. It's when a company sits down and thinks really hard about where they want to go and how they're going to get there. They make a big plan with lots of steps, just like you would on your treasure quest. It helps them make sure they're heading in the right direction and have everything they need for their journey!

Streamline

Alright, let's pretend you have a bunch of different toys in your room. Some are for building, some are for drawing, and some are for playing games. But sometimes, it's hard to find exactly what you want because they're all mixed up.

Streamlining in business is a bit like organizing your toys. Imagine you put all your building toys in one box, your drawing stuff in another, and your games in another. Now, when you want to build something, you can go right to your building toy box and find what you need. It makes everything easier and faster! In a company, streamlining means organizing things so they can work more smoothly and efficiently.

Subchapter T Corporation

Imagine you and your friends decide to build a clubhouse together. But you realize that everyone has different ideas about how it should be done. Some want a slide, some want a treehouse, and others want a cool secret door.

A Subchapter T Corporation is a bit like that clubhouse project. It's a special type of company where a group of people come together to do business. Each person has a say in how things are run, kind of like how your friends have a say in what goes into the clubhouse. It's a way for everyone to work together and make decisions about the company.

Succession Planning

Let's imagine you have a big box of colorful crayons. You use them to draw amazing pictures and share them with your friends. But sometimes, you need to leave and go do something else, like have dinner or go to bed.

Succession planning is a bit like that. It's when grown-ups in a company think about who will take over their important jobs when they need to leave or do something else. They choose and train someone to step in and keep things going just like you might pass on your crayons to a friend to continue the fun artwork. It helps make sure everything runs smoothly even when the original person isn't there.

Supply Chain

Alright, let's pretend you're the captain of a fantastical candy-making factory! You're in charge of creating the most delicious candies in the whole wide world. But wait, you can't do it all by yourself! You need different ingredients, like sugar, chocolate, and some magical flavors, right?

Now, imagine these ingredients don't just appear out of thin air. They come from different places, like sugar farms, cocoa bean plantations, and special flavor factories. They travel all the way to your candy factory through a magical network of candy delivery ships and candy trucks!

This entire process, from gathering the ingredients to bringing them to your factory, is like a big, interconnected adventure. This adventure of getting all the pieces you need to make your amazing candies is what we call a "supply chain" in the business world. It's the journey of all the different things coming together so you can create your sweet masterpieces!

Supply Chain Management

Let's pretend you're the leader of a team building a super cool fort in your backyard. You've got different stations for different jobs. One friend is in charge of collecting all the building materials, like blankets and pillows. Another friend is responsible for making sure there's enough snacks and drinks for everyone. And of course, someone's got to make sure everyone knows what they're doing and that everything fits together just right.

Well, in a big company, there's something like this fort-building team called the "Supply Chain Management." It's all about making sure that everything needed to make and sell a product, like the materials and parts, get to the right places at the right times. It's like making sure all the pieces for your awesome fort are gathered and ready for building!

SWOT Analysis (Strengths, Weaknesses, Opportunities, Threats)

Alright, let's play a game where we're secret agents trying to solve a mystery! We have a special tool called a "SWOT Analysis" to help us. Imagine it's like having a special gadget that helps us figure out our strengths, weaknesses, opportunities, and threats.

- **Strengths**: These are like our super cool spy skills, things we're really good at, like being great at puzzles or super fast runners.
- **Weaknesses**: These are like the challenges we face, like maybe we're not very good at keeping secrets or sometimes we get scared easily.
- **Opportunities**: These are chances for us to do something awesome, like finding a secret passageway or a clue that leads us to the next part of the mission.
- **Threats**: These are things that might try to stop us, like tricky traps set by the bad guys or a time limit to solve the mystery.

So, the SWOT Analysis is like our special agent tool that helps us plan and figure out how to tackle the mission. It's like having a map and a plan to make sure we're ready for anything that comes our way!

Synergize

Imagine you and your friends are putting on a play. Each of you has a special role to play, like one person is the main character, one is in charge of the cool props, and another is in charge of the music. Now, if each person does their job really well, the play will be amazing!

When you all work together smoothly and make the play even better because you're cooperating, that's like "synergizing" in a company. It means everyone brings their unique talents and skills to the table to create something really awesome together. It's like when musicians in a band all play their instruments at the same time to make a great song!

Synergy

Let's say you and your friends decide to build a really cool treehouse. One friend is great at designing, another is good with tools, and the third is awesome at finding cool decorations.

Now, if each of you worked separately, you might end up with three okay treehouses. But when you all work together and combine your skills, something amazing happens! You build a treehouse that's way better than anything you could have made alone. That special power when you all work together and create something awesome, that's what we call "synergy" in the corporate world. It's like when a team in a soccer game works together really well to score an incredible goal!

Take it Offline

Let's say you and your friends are playing a big game of tag at the park. But suddenly, one friend has a question about a totally different game they want to play later. Instead of stopping the whole tag game to talk about it, your friend says, "Hey, let's take it offline!" This means they'll talk about it later, after all the excitement of the tag game has settled down. It's like pausing a video game to check the controls – you deal with it later so you can keep having fun in the moment!

Take it to the Next Level

Okay, imagine you're playing a video game, like a really cool adventure game. You've mastered the easy levels and collected a bunch of treasures. But now, it's time to face even bigger challenges and discover even cooler stuff! Taking it to the next level at work means you've done really well at what you were doing, and now it's time to tackle something even more exciting and important. It's like going from being a skilled knight to becoming the legendary hero who saves the whole kingdom!

Talent Acquisition

Alright, think of talent acquisition like a big puzzle. Imagine you're putting together a puzzle with lots of different pieces. Each piece represents a special skill or talent that a company needs to do its job really well. The job of the talent acquisition team is to find all these special puzzle pieces and bring them to the company. They make sure the company has all the right skills in its team to do amazing things, just like having all the right puzzle pieces makes a beautiful picture!

Target Audience

Let's talk about a target audience. Imagine you're a super cool magician doing a magic show. You've got all these amazing tricks up your sleeve, right? But you also know that not everyone will be equally amazed by all your tricks.

So, before your show, you figure out who your special audience is. Are they mostly kids who love colorful tricks? Or are they grown-ups who like mind-boggling illusions? By understanding who's watching, you can tailor your show to make sure everyone has the most magical time possible! In the same way, in business, companies figure out who their target audience is so they can offer them exactly what they want. It's like making sure the right people get to see the coolest magic tricks!

Target Market

Let's imagine you're a brilliant author, named Aristotle, and you've just finished writing an incredible adventure story. Now, who do you think would enjoy this story the most? Would it be astronauts who love space adventures, or maybe wizards and witches who enjoy magical quests?

Your "target market" is like the group of people who would really, really love your story. So, when you publish your book, you'd want to tell astronauts about it, or maybe send a special message to the wizards and witches, right? That way, the right people will get to read and enjoy your amazing adventure! In business, companies think about their target market just like you do with your stories. They figure out who will love their products or services the most, and then they make sure those are the people who hear about them!

Tax Law Firms

Alright, let's talk about tax law firms. Imagine you're playing a really big and complicated board game. This game has a bunch of rules, and you need to make sure you follow them all to play properly. But sometimes, there are rules that are a bit tricky to understand.

So, you ask for help from someone who's an expert at this game. They know all the rules inside and out. They're like a super knowledgeable guide who can explain everything and make sure you're playing by the book. Tax law firms are a bit like those expert guides, but for grown-ups dealing with really complex rules about money and taxes. They help people understand and follow all the tax rules so they don't accidentally make mistakes!

Tenant

Let's talk about tenants. Imagine you have a big, delicious pizza. You own the pizza, and it's in your pizza box. But maybe you can't eat the whole pizza by yourself, so you decide to share it with your friends.

Now, imagine your friends are like tenants. They get a slice of the pizza, and while they're eating it, they're staying in your pizza party zone. They don't own the whole pizza box, but they get to enjoy a part of it for a little while. In a building, a tenant is like someone who gets to stay in a space (like an apartment or a shop) that belongs to someone else, and they usually pay rent for the privilege. They're like the pizza party guests in your pizza box!

Think Outside the Box

Alright, let's talk about "Thinking Outside the Box." Imagine you have a treasure chest. Normally, people expect to find gold and jewels inside. But you, being super clever, decide to use the treasure chest as a fancy pet house for your adventurous parrot.

See, while everyone else is looking inside the chest for treasures, you thought in a totally different way and found a whole new use for it! That's what "Thinking Outside the Box" means in the grown-up world. It's about coming up with creative and different ideas that others might not have thought of. It's like using a treasure chest for a parrot house instead of just storing treasure!

Thought Leader

Imagine you're in a class, and there's a student who always comes up with the coolest ideas for projects. When it's time for the class to pick a topic for a big presentation, everyone turns to this student for suggestions because they know this student has great thoughts and ideas.

In the grown-up world, a "Thought Leader" is like that super smart and creative kid in your class. They're the person that others look up to for new and innovative ideas. People trust them to lead the way with their fresh and clever thinking. They're like the idea experts of the group!

Thought Shower

Think of a "Thought Shower" like a brainstorming session, but with a fun twist. Imagine you and your friends want to plan the best summer vacation ever. Instead of just sitting around and thinking, "Where should we go?" you decide to have a "Thought Shower."

During a "Thought Shower," you all gather in a room, and it's like standing under a magical rain cloud of ideas. Everyone starts sharing their wildest and coolest vacation ideas without worrying about how silly or impossible they might sound. You might suggest going to the moon or having a roller coaster in the middle of the ocean!

In the grown-up world, a "Thought Shower" is when people get together to share lots of creative ideas about a project or problem. Just like your fun brainstorming session for the perfect vacation, they're trying to come up with exciting and imaginative solutions without any limitations. It's like a burst of creative raindrops that help generate fantastic ideas!

Title

Think of a "Title" like a special badge you earn when you become really, really good at something. Imagine you're in a magical school of wizards and you've just become the best potion-maker. The wise headmaster gives you the "Master Potion-Maker" title. This means you're the go-to expert for making amazing potions!

In the world of grown-ups, getting a "Title" works in a similar way. When someone is super-duper good at their job, they might get a special name or title to show how awesome they are at it. For example, imagine a person who's incredibly good at drawing and making beautiful pictures. They might get the title of "Master Illustrator" or "Artistic Wizard" at their workplace! This title is like a shiny badge that tells everyone, "This person is amazing at what they do!"

Title Insurance

Imagine you have a very special treasure map, and it shows you where a hidden treasure chest full of gold and jewels is buried. But, there's a problem! What if the map isn't quite right, and you accidentally dig in the wrong spot? You'd be pretty disappointed, right?

Title insurance is like having a magical map checker. When someone buys a piece of land (like a backyard or a field), they get a special document called a "title" that says they own it. But sometimes, there might be a mistake in the title, just like there could be a mistake on a treasure map.

Title insurance is like having a wizard who checks the map (or title) to make sure it's right. If there's a mistake, the title insurance helps fix it, so the person can be sure they really own the land they bought. It's like having a backup plan to make sure everything is fair and correct!

Tokenization

Alright, let's imagine you have a big jar of colorful marbles. Each marble represents something special, like a toy or a treat. Now, imagine you want to share these marbles with your friends, but it's not easy to split them up evenly.

Tokenization is a bit like turning each of these marbles into a special coin that represents the same value. So, you can give your friends these coins, and they can exchange them for marbles later. This way, everyone can enjoy the treats or toys equally, and it's much easier to share!

Total Quality Management (TQM)

Imagine you're the captain of a pirate ship. You've got a crew that helps you sail and find treasure. Now, you want to make sure that everything on your ship works perfectly. That's where Total Quality Management, or TQM, comes in.

It's like having a special crew member whose only job is to make sure all the sails are in perfect shape, the cannons are clean and ready, and the ship is sailing smoothly. This way, you can be sure that your ship is always in top-notch condition and ready for any adventure!

Touch Base

Think of a game of tag with your friends. When you need to rest or talk about a plan, you might all gather around a special spot, like a big tree, and have a quick chat. This "touch base" moment helps everyone get on the same page and make sure everyone knows what's going on in the game. In business, when people say they need to "touch base," it's like saying they need a quick meeting to make sure everyone is on the same page about a project or plan.

Trade Secret

Imagine you have a secret recipe for making the most amazing chocolate chip cookies. It's so special that you don't want anyone else to know about it. You keep it hidden in a special secret drawer in your kitchen. Well, in companies, they also have special things they do or make that give them an edge over others. These are called "trade secrets." They're like super-secret recipes that help the company do something really well, and they keep them locked up tight so nobody else can use them!

Trademark

Let's say you have a special sticker that you put on all your favorite toys. This sticker tells everyone that these toys belong to you and they're super special. It's like your own personal mark! In companies, they have something similar called a "trademark." It's like a special sign or symbol that they put on their products to show that they made them. So when you see that mark, you know it's from that company! It's like your sticker, but for grown-up stuff.

Training and Development

Alright, imagine you're a superhero in training. You've got your special costume, but you need to learn all the cool moves, right? So, you go to a special school just for superheroes. There, they teach you how to fly, use your super strength, and even how to control your awesome powers. This school is like the "Training and Development" department in a company. It's where the employees go to learn new skills and get even better at their jobs. Just like a superhero school helps heroes become even more amazing, the Training and Development department helps employees become super skilled at their jobs!

Transparency

Pretend you're the captain of a pirate ship, and you've just found a big treasure chest filled with shiny gold coins. You want to share this treasure with your whole crew because you're a fair and honest captain.

Being "transparent" in the corporate world is a bit like you being open and honest about how much treasure you found. You show your crew exactly what's inside the chest, and you explain how you'll divide it up. Everyone knows what's going on, and they trust you because you're not hiding anything.

In business, when a company is transparent, it means they're open and honest about what they're doing. They share information about their plans, how they're doing financially, and how they treat their employees and customers. Just like you with your pirate crew, this helps build trust with everyone involved!

Turnkey

Imagine you have a magic box. When you open it, everything you need for a fantastic adventure pops out - maps, tools, snacks, and even a cool hat! You don't have to worry about finding or making anything yourself. It's like a ready-made adventure kit!

In the business world, when someone offers a "turnkey solution," it means they're giving you everything you need for a project or task, just like that magic adventure box. You don't have to go searching for all the pieces; they're all provided, making things much easier and faster!

Unique Selling Proposition (USP)

Alright, let's think about superheroes!

Imagine there are a bunch of superheroes in a big city, and they all have their own special powers. Now, let's say there's one superhero who can do something really amazing that none of the others can do. Maybe they have the power to fly faster than a rocket or lift buildings with their pinky finger!

That superhero's special power is like a company's "Unique Selling Proposition" or USP. It's the thing that makes them stand out from all the others. Just like this superhero has a power that no one else has, a company's USP is the special thing they do or offer that's different and super cool compared to all the other companies out there.

So, a Unique Selling Proposition is like a superhero's special power that makes them unique in the world of superheroes! It's what makes a company special in the world of businesses.

Value Add

Let's imagine you have a plain sandwich. It's got bread and some cheese inside, but it's missing something special to make it really delicious. Now, let's say you add some crispy, golden-brown bacon to that sandwich. Suddenly, it's not just any sandwich, it's an extra tasty, extra special sandwich!

That crispy bacon is like the "value add" in a business. It's that extra something that makes a product or service even better and more valuable. Just like the bacon turns a plain sandwich into something amazing, a "value add" makes a product or service stand out and be even more awesome!

Value Chain

Imagine you're a pizza chef, and you want to make the best pizza in the world. You first buy the book collection called "The Book of Flavors". Then you start by growing the juiciest tomatoes, making the freshest cheese, and baking the crunchiest crust.

Now, think of each step in making that pizza as a link in a chain. Each link, from growing the tomatoes to baking the crust, adds value to your pizza. If any link in the chain isn't top-notch, your pizza won't be as delicious as it could be.

In business, a "value chain" is like all the steps a company takes to create and deliver a product or service. Just like with your pizza, each step adds value. If any step isn't done well, it can affect the overall quality of what the company offers. So, understanding the value chain helps companies make sure they're doing every step right!

Value Proposition

Imagine you and your friends are trading stickers. You have a really special sticker that's shiny, colorful, and has a cool design. Now, your friend offers you two regular stickers in exchange for your special one. You think about it and realize that your special sticker is worth more than the two regular ones.

In this sticker trade, your special sticker is like a "value proposition" in business. It means what makes something special and worth more compared to other things. So, when a company talks about its value proposition, they're saying why their product or service is extra special and better than what others might offer. It's like saying, "Our stickers are so cool, they're worth more than just any regular sticker!"

Variable Costs

Alright! Let's think about making cookies. Imagine you're going to bake some delicious cookies, and you have all the ingredients in your kitchen. Now, here's the interesting part: some ingredients, like flour, sugar, and eggs, you use a little bit of each time you make a batch of cookies. These are like "variable costs."

But there are other things, like the baking tray and the mixing bowl, that you don't use up or change every time you bake. You just wash them and use them again. These are more like "fixed costs" because they stay the same no matter how many cookies you make.

So, when a company talks about variable costs, they're talking about the things they use up a little bit each time they make something, like ingredients for cookies. It's important for them to keep track of these costs to know how much they're spending on each batch of what they're making.

Vendor

Let's pretend you're throwing a big birthday party. You want to have lots of fun games and delicious snacks. But, there's a little challenge. You don't have all the games and snacks at your house. So, what do you do?

You decide to ask some friendly neighbors if they can help. One neighbor lends you a cool game, and another neighbor shares some yummy treats. These helpful neighbors are like your vendors! They provide you with things you need to make your party awesome.

In the business world, a vendor is like a special friend who provides a company with the things it needs to do its job. It could be supplies, like paper and pencils for an office, or ingredients for a restaurant. Vendors are like the unsung heroes who help businesses run smoothly!

Vendor Management

Let's imagine you're hosting a big party with lots of fun activities. Now, you want to make sure you have all the supplies you need, like balloons, games, and snacks. But, you don't have everything at home, so you need to ask different people or stores to provide them.

So, you become like the party planner, and the people or stores that provide the supplies are your "vendors." You talk to them, negotiate prices, and make sure they bring everything on time. It's kind of like when a company works with different vendors to get all the things they need to make their products or run their business smoothly. It's important to manage these vendors well, just like you'd want to make sure your party supplies are just right for your guests!

Venture Capitalist (VC)

Imagine you have a super cool idea for a brand new board game. You know it's going to be a hit, but you need some help to make it happen. That's where a "venture capitalist" comes in. They're like someone who has a bunch of gold coins and they're looking for awesome ideas to invest in.

So, you go to the venture capitalist and you say, "Hey, I've got this incredible board game idea, but I need some gold coins to make it real." The venture capitalist listens carefully and thinks, "Hmm, this sounds like a fun and exciting game that could make a lot of people happy."

If they like your idea, they might give you some of their gold coins to help bring your game to life. In return, they'll own a part of the game, kind of like being a co-creator. If your game becomes super popular, everyone gets to share in the fun and success! That's how a venture capitalist works in the grown-up world of businesses and ideas. They help bring cool stuff into the world!

Vertical Integration

Let's imagine you love baking cookies. You start with the most important ingredient: the cookie dough. Now, you have two options. You can either buy the dough from the store, or you can make it yourself.

If you decide to make the dough at home, you're doing something called vertical integration. It's like becoming your own cookie dough maker instead of depending on someone else to do it. This way, you have more control over the entire cookie-making process, from start to finish! In business, companies might choose to do this too, like making their own parts instead of buying them from others.

Vesting Period

Alright, let's imagine you're in a really fun club with your friends, and you all have special badges that make you part of the club. But here's the thing: to keep your badge and all the special benefits, you need to stay in the club for a certain amount of time. This period of time is like a "vesting period."

It's kind of like saying, "Hey, if you want to keep your super cool club badge and all the cool stuff that comes with it, you have to be a member for at least a year." This way, it encourages everyone to stick around and enjoy all the fun things the club has to offer! In the grown-up world, a vesting period works in a similar way for certain perks and benefits at work. It's like earning your special badge for being part of the team!

Virtual Organization

Let's imagine you're a superhero, and you have a secret base where you plan all your missions. Now, what if your superhero friends from all around the world also had their own secret bases, and you needed to work together to save the day? That would be really cool, right?

A virtual organization is a bit like that. It's when a group of people from different places work together as if they were all in the same office, even though they're actually far away. They use special tools on their computers to talk, share ideas, and get things done, just like you and your superhero friends would use your gadgets to communicate and save the world!

Virtual Team

Let's imagine you're the captain of a super cool spaceship, and you have a team of astronauts. But here's the twist: your team members aren't all in the same spaceship with you. They're in different spaceships all over the galaxy!

Now, even though they're not in the same spaceship as you, you all have special devices that let you talk, send messages, and work together like you're side by side. So, you can still complete missions and explore new planets, even if you're far away from each other.

That's a bit like a virtual team. It's a group of people who work together on projects, but they might be in different cities or even different countries. They use special tools on their computers to talk, share ideas, and get things done, just like you and your spaced-out team of astronauts!

Visibility

Let's imagine you're playing a game of hide-and-seek with your friends, but instead of just hiding, you have to wear these super cool glow-in-the-dark stickers. When you're wearing them, everyone can see you, no matter where you're hiding!

Now, think of visibility in a company like those glow-in-the-dark stickers. When a company has good visibility, it means everyone can see what's going on. Like, imagine if all the workers knew what their jobs were, and the bosses knew how well everyone was doing. It's like everyone has those special stickers on, and they can see what's happening all around!

Vision Statement

Let's pretend we're on a big adventure! Imagine you and your friends are planning a trip to a magical island. Each of you has a special map that shows what you hope to find and do there. These maps are like your "vision statements" for the trip.

Your vision statement might say, "I want to find hidden treasures" or "I want to meet friendly creatures." It's like a special message that reminds you of what's really important during the adventure. In a company, a vision statement is a special message that reminds everyone of what they're working towards, kind of like the map for your magical island adventure!

Whistleblower

Alright, let's pretend you and your friends are playing a game, and one of your friends accidentally does something that's against the rules. They don't realize it, but you do. You have a choice to make: do you keep quiet, or do you blow the whistle and let everyone know what happened?

If you decide to blow the whistle, it means you're being like a "whistleblower." In the grown-up world, a whistleblower is someone who sees something wrong happening in a company or organization, and they speak up about it to make sure everyone knows. It's like being a rule keeper, but for grown-ups and companies! They're like the heroes who help keep things fair and right.

White Collar Crime

Pretend there's a group of people who work in an office, wearing their nice white-collar shirts. They're all really smart and good at what they do. But, imagine some of them start doing sneaky things behind the scenes. Maybe they're taking office supplies or even doing things that are against the rules.

This sneaky behavior is what we call "white collar crime." It's kind of like when someone in a game starts bending the rules to their advantage. In the grown-up world, white collar crime happens when people in offices or businesses do things that are not allowed, like cheating or being dishonest, but without getting their hands dirty like in other types of crimes. It's important to stop this kind of behavior, just like we'd stop someone from cheating in a game!

White Collared Worker

Imagine a big office building with lots of grown-ups going inside every day. These grown-ups are like the captains of a ship, steering the company in the right direction.

Now, think of them as the brainiacs of the team. They wear clean, white collared shirts and sit at desks with computers, just like a scientist in a lab coat. They use their minds to come up with all sorts of ideas, make important decisions, and figure out how to make the company better.

So, when we talk about a "white collared worker" in the grown-up world, we're talking about people who use their brains, ideas, and plans to help a company succeed. They're like the clever scientists of a big office adventure!

Win-Win

Alright, let's imagine you and your friend both have your favorite toys, and you really want to play with each other's toys. But there's a problem - you both want to keep your own toys too. Now, a "win-win" situation is when you come up with a clever idea. You decide to trade toys for a little while!

This way, both of you get to enjoy playing with something different, and you both feel happy about it. It's a win for you, and it's also a win for your friend. So, a "win-win" in business is like finding a way for everyone to be happy and satisfied with the outcome!

Win-Win Situation

Picture this: Imagine you and your friend both really want to play different games. You have a cool board game, and your friend has an awesome video game. But here's the thing - you both want to play your own games and have a great time.

Now, a "win-win situation" is like magic! You come up with an idea where you take turns playing. First, you have a blast with the video game, and then you switch to the board game. It's a win for you because you get to try something new, and it's also a win for your friend because they get to play their favorite game too. Everyone's happy! That's what a "win-win situation" is in business - when everyone involved gets something they want and feels good about it!

Working Capital

Alright, let's go on an adventure with your favorite trading cards! Imagine you have a collection of special cards, and you want to use them to play exciting games with your friends.

Now, some of these cards are super rare and powerful, while others are more common. The number of rare cards you have compared to the more common ones is like your "working capital." It's the special stuff you can use right away to have amazing battles and trade for new cards.

So, if you have lots of rare cards, it's like having a big supply of working capital. You can make big moves in your games and have loads of fun. But if you only have a few, you'll have to be more careful and strategic with how you play.

In business, working capital is like having a stockpile of resources (like money and assets) ready to use. The more you have, the more boldly you can make moves and seize opportunities!

Working Capital Turnover

Imagine you have a big jar filled with your favorite candies. This jar represents all the special resources a company has, like money, supplies, and equipment. Now, every time you take out a candy and use it for something important, it's like the company using a bit of its resources to do its work.

Working Capital Turnover is like how fast you use up those candies from your jar. If you take them out quickly, it means the company is using its resources effectively and getting a lot done. But if you take them out slowly, it might mean the company could be using its resources more efficiently.

So, it's like seeing how fast your candy jar empties out, and that tells you how well the company is putting its resources to good use!

Zoning

Let's imagine a big play area. There are different parts for different activities - one for running around, one for playing games, and another for reading books quietly.

Zoning in a company is a bit like this play area. It's when you decide which parts of the space are used for different things. For example, some areas might be for making things, others for offices, and some for meeting rooms.

Just like in our play area, where each part has a specific purpose, zoning helps companies organize their space so everyone can do their jobs effectively!

* * *

We would love to hear from **all of you** who supported this book!

Your **positive review** on *Amazon* would not only mean a lot to us, but it would also help other readers discover the book and embark on their own culinary adventure.

All it takes is just a minute to make a difference!

8

Conclusion

Congratulations, Future Business Leaders!

You've just completed an incredible journey through the world of corporate terminology, equipped with a wealth of knowledge that will be your companion for years to come. Take a moment to revel in your newfound expertise!

Parents and Educators, a huge thank you for joining us on this exciting adventure. Your support and guidance are crucial in nurturing these young minds into astute business enthusiasts.

Students, give yourselves a hearty pat on the back! You've conquered concepts that even some adults find tricky. You're now well on your way to becoming true business experts.

As you step forward, carry these business lessons with you. You're the trailblazers, the *SMEs* (Subject Matter Experts), of your generation. Imagine the impact you'll have on the business world!

Remember, every decision you make, whether big or small, involves a business aspect. With your newfound knowledge, you have the ability to make those decisions wisely and shape your business future.

Keep exploring, keep asking questions, and keep seeking opportunities to expand your business understanding. Share what you've learned with friends and family, and be ready to offer a helping hand when someone needs business advice.

And always remember, your business journey is just beginning. With each step, you're constructing a sturdy foundation for a future filled with business confidence and success.

So go forth, Future Business Leaders! The world is yours to conquer, armed with the knowledge that will set you apart in high school, college, and beyond. You're well on your way to a future where business decisions are made with clarity and confidence.

Thank you for being part of this amazing adventure. Keep shaping your business destiny, one smart choice at a time!

About the Author

The creative mind behind the '*Mind Shaping*' books, a line of literature devoted to improving lives through wisdom and insight, is **Aristotle**, a contemporary philosopher and genuine polymath.

Aristotle is not just an insightful thinker, but also a creative genius who is always coming up with new ideas and designs. His drive to explore new ideas is evidenced by his attempts to patent and market his inventions, which highlight his innovative spirit. Aristotle has always thought that information has the ability to influence how we live. He has set out on a mission to assist individuals in reshaping their minds and, as a result, their destinies. He has a plethora of experiences and a great grasp of life's complexities.

Aristotle has always been a source of wisdom, offering friends and students enlightening counsel that has changed their lives.Many owe his leadership and advice for helping them have better futures.

Aristotle ponders the nature of existence and shares his profound discoveries through his writings because he is passionate about learning what people really need. He thinks that a healthy mind may affect anything, including one's physical health, future prosperity, and beyond.

The commitment to lifelong learning shown by Aristotle is unmatched. His wide-ranging interests, which include project management, eastern medicine, real estate, and life insurance, are a reflection of his unquenchable curiosity. Aristotle speaks four languages casually and is a competent musician who plays the guitar, piano, and drums. His skills are as varied as his hobbies.

Aristotle has a variety of experience working in several financial institutions, including tech centers, bank teller positions, primary admin, and software engineering.

Aristotle is now keen to spread his knowledge by publishing '*Mind Shaping*' books. His books serve as a tribute to his dedication to assisting others in realizing their full potential by altering their thinking and setting out on a path to a better future.

Also by Aristotle

Unlock the secrets of idiomatic expressions with *"**Ultimate Idioms and Expressions Guide: 400+ Common Phrases Explained.**"* This comprehensive guide unravels the stories, meanings, and cultural contexts behind over 400 phrases, providing fresh insights and a deeper appreciation for the rich tapestry of human communication.

Delve into the origins, contexts, and cultural nuances of each idiom, gaining a profound understanding of their usage. This book is an indispensable resource for language enthusiasts, students, writers, and anyone curious about the fascinating world of idiomatic language.

Foreign schools and students learning English as a second language will find this guide an essential reference and study aid for understanding English idioms and mastering colloquial expressions.

Published by Marble Publishers: Eternal Prose 2023

Ultimate Idioms and Expressions Guide: 400+ Common Phrases Explained

Embark on a transformative journey through language with "*Ultimate Idioms and Expressions Guide: 400+ Common Phrases Explained.*" This comprehensive guide unlocks the stories, meanings, and cultural contexts behind each phrase, offering invaluable insights for a deeper understanding of human communication.

Perfect for those seeking clarity on intricate idiomatic expressions, this resource is essential for anyone who has struggled to decipher certain phrases. It's an indispensable reference for learners of English as a second language, providing a solid foundation in understanding and utilizing colloquial expressions.

www.ingramcontent.com/pod-product-compliance
Lightning Source LLC
Chambersburg PA
CBHW072149290526
45794CB00004B/1462

* 9 7 9 8 8 6 3 1 0 0 4 8 7 *